BETWEEN FREEDOM AND NECESSITY

An Essay on the Place of Value

Steven Schroeder

Rodopi

Amsterdam - Atlanta, GA 2000

The paper on which this book is printed meets the requirements of "ISO 9706:1994, Information and documentation - Paper for documents - Requirements for permanence".

ISBN: 90-420-1302-8
©Editions Rodopi B.V., Amsterdam - Atlanta, GA 2000
Printed in The Netherlands

…what then, indeed,
If mortals are not greater by the head
Than any of their propensities? what then,
Unless the artist keep up open roads
Betwixt the seen and unseen, - bursting through
The best of your conventions with his best.

Elizabeth Barrett Browning, *Aurora Leigh*

CONTENTS

viii   CONTENTS

FOREWORD

Value inquiry takes in a number of fields of thought on matters of value, disciplinary fields such as ethics, aesthetics, and economics. Certainly the disciplinary fields may be explored individually and in detail with the eye of a specialist. They may also be viewed for formal features of value that they may share, an activity of meta-disciplinary value inquiry that itself calls for a certain type of specialization. But value inquiry may also bring together reflections from several disciplinary fields for insights that they may provide on one or more of them. This is interdisciplinary value inquiry, an activity that cuts across areas of specialization. It is the activity that Steven Schroeder is engaged in here. He has essayed a thought-provoking work on ethics which is not limited to discussions of ethics.

If the very notion of ethics presupposes the possibility of freedom of action, then the realm of moral value is bounded by the limits to liberty, necessity, and chance. Within those bounds lies a broad range of conduct, more or less subject to suggestion, direction, guiding, goading, restraint, and constraint. Some incursions on freedom are inevitable in order to live well, and even, odd as it sounds, for their instrumental value in extending freedom. The limits that property rights impose on what we might do, make it possible for us to dispose as we decidedly want to do. Traffic lights that regulate the actions of drivers increase the prospect of crossing intersections free of collisions, even in New York. Of course this may go too far, with imposition and regulation in the name of freedom coming at too high a cost to freedom itself or to other values.

It should be plain that a broad range of conduct can enter into discussions of ethics. The conduct may be affected by moral values, even if the moral influence is not always as great as it should be. But the conduct may also be affected by all manner of other values, whether aesthetic, economic, pedagogic, historic, scientific, or religious. Steven Schroeder considers values, or dimensions of value, of all these types in discussing issues of moral concern. His multifaceted approach will engage an active reader. May it also spur more forays in interdisciplinary value inquiry.

Thomas Magnell
Drew University

PREFACE

You cannot tell people what to do, you can only tell them parables; and that is what art really is, particular stories of particular people and experiences.
W.H. Auden (Spears, 1963)

This fragment of philosophy joins an old conversation at the intersection of freedom and necessity. Intersections invite roadmaps. Because so much current popular discussion makes "freedom" and "necessity" polar opposites on a single continuum of individual will, this intersection will carry us into territory that may prove unfamiliar though it is hardly unexplored.

In earlier versions of the conversation, freedom and necessity are not opposites but equally important and intimately connected ingredients involved in formation and exercise of will. To say that freedom and necessity are cast as polar opposites on a continuum of individual will is a reminder that the language of necessity is often used in contemporary conversation to exclude freedom and absolve actors of moral responsibility, while the language of freedom is often used to exclude necessity and transform moral discussion into a competition of individual whims. These exclusions are recent innovations that have had a profoundly negative impact on moral reasoning and moral discourse. Reaching back before the exclusions is a modest attempt at course correction.

I called the conversation an old one. Here I draw on material from some of the earliest sources in Western thought, including the classical tradition in Greek philosophy represented by Plato and Aristotle and the classical tradition in Greek tragic drama represented by Aeschylus, Sophocles, and Euripides. Both of these classical traditions draw on earlier mythic material systematized in the poetry of Homer, who may himself be a partly fictional literary device designed to hold that material together in a form that could be addressed by the traditions of philosophy and tragic drama. Each of those traditions is populated by characters who are participants in this conversation: Agamemnon, Antigone, Creon, and Hecuba as surely as Protagoras and Socrates. In my exposition of the conversation, I draw especially on two contemporary philosophers, Alasdair MacIntyre and Martha Nussbaum, and one not quite so contemporary, Søren Kierkegaard, who have devoted great care to interpretation of classical traditions as they relate to ethics.

At this point, the content of the tradition is less important than the form of the conversation. The form is generalizable in some important ways: a mythic tradition with partially obscured origins first becomes submerged in the consciousness of a people and a place as reflected in the stories of that people and place. These stories become the subject of critical reflection in a variety of local forms, ranging from oral discourse through poetry and drama to formal philosophical speculation. That critical reflection itself becomes the subject of criticism in the multilayered conversation characteristic of philosophy. The conversation is composed of myth, characters who transform myth into poetry and song, characters who populate poetry and song, critical appropriation of myth in dramas and speculative essays that relentlessly probe problematic dimensions of human existence, and critical reflection on the appropriation.

Note that the form is locative, even where the content does not settle in one place. Stories are stories of particular people and places, and conversation about universals has been folded into particular stories in the West as surely as elsewhere, even when the West has staked its identity on denial of particularity. Taking up an image that was of critical importance to Kierkegaard in the middle of the nineteenth century, folding the conversation into particular stories means that there is "no disciple at second hand." We address participants in the conversation as present, not as frozen relics excavated from an inaccessible past and not primarily as characters in an historical narrative.

The classical traditions to which I have already referred are fascinated with the necessity of free action and, more specifically, the forging of freedom out of necessity. It is not surprising that this fascination is taken up in the eighteenth and nineteenth-century European philosophy that provides a background for human rights conversation today. Both periods are marked by rapidly developing conceptions of Nature and humanity's place in Nature. As the so-called Industrial Revolution gained momentum in nineteenth-century Britain, the mechanization of Nature, including humanity, became a central concern of philosophers as well as poets. The confrontation with machines that begins in earnest in nineteenth-century Britain often echoes the earlier confrontation with fate in classical Greece.

This is the rationale for the primary cast of characters in this extended essay, which, though it takes place at the beginning of the twenty-first century by the "Christian" reckoning that has become an integral part of European identity, will at times read like a conversation between classical Greece and nineteenth-century Europe. The cast consists of characters drawn from Aeschylus, Sophocles, Euripides, and Plato as well as the authors themselves—Plato, Aristotle, Locke, Hume, Kant, Kierkegaard, MacIntyre, and Nussbaum. Some of these writers have been associated with displaced, displacing claims of universality; but each is in place and in time in ways that are instructive for ethics. Again, the form: myth, the matter of stories, becomes also the matter of critical reflection, which in turn is subjected to critical reflection. Every fragment of philosophy is a contribution to the reflection, and it is nothing if it is separated from the matter—the stories, the myths, and the characters (including us) who both make them and live in them.

ACKNOWLEDGMENTS

Much of the material presented here was developed in ethics classes that I taught during my four years as Associate Professor of Religion and Philosophy at Capital University's Dayton Center. I am grateful to students in those classes for their patience, their perceptive comments, and their questions as we worked through this material together. I am also grateful to colleagues at the Dayton Center and at the other campuses of Capital University for the collegial and supportive atmosphere they cultivated there. Andy Carlson, now Associate Dean and Director of the Center, has sustained a good argument regarding themes in this book from the first time I met him, and I am especially grateful for that. I thank Provost Ron Volpe and Dean Gary Smith for their enthusiastic support of travel to academic conferences where I could hone these ideas in conversation with a broader academic community.

I first covered some of the ground in Chapters Two, Three, Five, and Six in *Virginia Woolf's Subject and the Subject of Ethics* (Lewiston, N.Y.: Edwin Mellen Press, 1996). An earlier version of the first part of Chapter Four was presented at a meeting of the Society for Philosophy in the Contemporary World in Estes Park, Colorado, in August 1994 and published as "No Goddess Was Your Mother: Western Philosophy's Abandonment of Its Multicultural Matrix," in *Philosophy in the Contemporary World* 2.1 (Spring 1995), pp. 27-32. The discussion of Ed Reed's work in Chapter Five began as a presentation at the Twentieth World Congress of Philosophy in Boston in August 1998. I presented an early version of the discussion of culture and value in Chapter Six at a meeting of the International Society for Value Inquiry in Helsinki in August 1993. The discussion of entropy and art in Chapter Six began as a presentation at the Fifth International Conference on Persons in Santa Fe, New Mexico, in August 1999. The material in Chapter Nine was first presented at the Fourth International Conference on Persons in Prague in August 1997. Material in Chapters Ten and Eleven was first presented at meetings of the Midwest American Academy of Religion in Terre Haute and Valparaiso, Indiana. I also presented material in Chapter Eleven at the Sixth Annual International Bonhoeffer Conference at Union Theological Seminary in New York in August 1992 and to faculty and students at Capital University's Dayton Center in December 1996. A revised version of the presentation at Union appeared as "The End of History and the Responsibility to 'Order' the World: Dietrich Bonhoeffer and the 'New World Order'," in *Union Seminary Quarterly Review* 46.1-4 (1992), pp. 21-38, and was reprinted as "The End of History and the New World Order," in *Theology and the Practice of Responsibility: Essays on Dietrich Bonhoeffer*, Edited by Wayne Whitson Floyd, Jr. and Charles R. Marsh, Jr.

(Valley Forge, Penn.: Trinity Press International, 1994, pp. 21-38). I am grateful to all who responded to these earlier presentations. Their comments and criticisms have been invaluable in what is still an ongoing construction process.

One

WALKING BACKWARDS

Academic conversation almost always involves walking backwards. This may seem awkward, but it is not as strange as it first appears: almost anyone can quickly stir up a string of examples that involve similar behavior in non-academic settings.

Think of interactions between an adult and a young child who is just learning to walk. It is not at all uncommon to see the adult, face-to-face with the child, slowly backing up, coaxing one more step. Presumably, an adult is able to do this because she or he has achieved sufficient facility in walking so that it no longer requires the kind of concentrated physical and intellectual effort demanded of the child taking first steps. The adult's steps are no less complex than the child's, but, because the cognitive processes associated with taking them have dropped out of sight, she or he is able both to walk backwards and to attend to the process of the child's walking.

Or flash forward to the same adult teaching the same child to ride a bicycle. At some point in the process, the adult may stand in front of the bike, facing the child, holding the child's hands on the handlebars—walking backwards so the child can roll forward without falling.

Or consider an umpire in a game of baseball standing in shallow left field when a pop fly is hit over the shortstop's head. To avoid a collision without losing sight of the play, the umpire backpedals. The shortstop probably backpedals as well to avoid losing sight of the ball. There is a high degree of complexity and potential danger in this scenario. The shortstop running backwards and the left fielder running forward are converging on the spot where the ball is coming down, while the umpire running backwards is simultaneously avoiding the players and staying close enough to insure a good look at the play.

One thing these examples have in common is that the persons in each case who are walking or running backwards are doing it in order to keep an eye on what someone or something else is doing, not because it is a natural way to walk.

And there is the famous example of the dancer Ginger Rogers, who, as former Texas Governor Ann Richards reminded us in a nationally televised speech a few years ago, did everything her partner Fred Astaire did—only backwards and in high heels.

This last example highlights social and contextual aspects more clearly than the first three. In the first place, backwards in this case is relative: Fred and

Ginger were face to face (or, I suppose, cheek to cheek), and their dances did not move in a straight line. Ann Richards, no doubt, is aware of the political dimensions that define Fred into the lead and put Ginger dancing backwards in uncomfortable shoes. In the second place, this dance is relational: as they say, it takes two to tango. Isolate the adult from the child in the first two examples, and his or her backwards movement will appear decidedly eccentric. And, while the backpedaling of both umpire and shortstop appear perfectly appropriate under the conditions described in the third example, an umpire or a shortstop that always ran backwards would pose problems for the game.

Which brings me back to academic conversation. When I say that it involves walking backwards, I mean that it deliberately reverses ordinary experience by giving theory temporal precedence over practice.

1. From Is to Ought: The Place of Value

Academic discourse is sometimes encountered in a distorted form that is not a conversation at all, but a one-way dispensation of theory—from the head of the teacher into the head of the student. This is ballroom dancing without a partner, not recommended as a technique for dancing or for learning.

In ordinary experience, theory emerges out of practice and is usually submerged in its smooth execution. Academic conversation often reverses this by starting with theory. In this case, walking backwards involves reconnecting particular theories with particular practices out of which they emerged. This acknowledges the descriptive function of theory and may help us, like the umpire, get a good look at the play. That is a legitimate task, but it is not the whole story. Theories are almost always put to prescriptive use as well, most effectively when they are most thoroughly submerged.

The dancer dancing backwards may not be able to articulate a theory of dancing and would probably not be well served as a dancer by the attempt to do so. Less dramatically, the walker walking backwards would probably be hard-pressed even to describe the process of walking forward. Articulating such a description would be a distraction that might very well cause both dancer and walker to stumble. To walk or dance smoothly requires that theory be completely integrated into practice.

If an accomplished dancer becomes a choreographer, this can be both strength and weakness. The dancer may tease a theory out of his or her practice, but what does that theory have to do with somebody else's dance?

It may become prescriptive in a number of ways, the most destructive of which would discourage creativity in the next generation of dancers and, in the long run, diminish the dance.

The shift from description to prescription—from is to ought—is essential to discussion of value, which in academic settings is most likely to occur under one of three rubrics: ethics, economics, or aesthetics. There may be reasons for distinguishing these as three different species of the genus value, but it would be a mistake to ignore the genus: what is common to all three, and what light does it shed on the relationship between description and prescription?

All three describe individual and social behavior and its results. Two of the three, ethics and economics, sometimes aspire to be described as sciences, while the third, aesthetics, rarely makes such a claim. One of the three, economics, sometimes aspires to be described as a natural rather than a social science.

These aspirations are interesting. They locate discussion of value in three contexts: in the humanities, on the border between the humanities and the social sciences, and on the border between the social and the natural sciences. Description of behavior and its results ranges from the human through the social to the natural, which are not mutually exclusive categories. Traditionally, that range has been understood as moving from freedom at the human end toward necessity at the natural end. This is likely reflected in the level of confidence at each of the three steps in the range: from aesthetics, where "there is no accounting for taste"; through ethics, where accounting is more often than not an argument; to economics, where there is nothing if not accounting. The least prescriptive of the three, and the one where description is most disputatious, is aesthetics. The most prescriptive, and the one where description is most homogeneous is economics.

2. Freedom and Necessity

This relationship between freedom and necessity is historically important for discussion of value. It is reflected in the ancient Greek division of philosophy into three sciences—physics, ethics, and logic—that Immanuel Kant (1724-1804) took up late in the eighteenth century in his discussion of moral philosophy. Kant divided knowledge into two categories, formal and material. Formal knowledge is the domain of logic, while material knowledge is the domain of ethics and physics. The matter of ethics is freedom, while the matter of physics is nature.

It would be unwise to surrender form without a struggle, but we can push that aside for a moment and attend to this matter of matter. Speaking the language of the European Enlightenment (as in "we hold these truths to be self-evident"), Kant assumes that all we have to do is look at the matter: if we see necessity, we are in the realm of natural science; if we see freedom, we are in the realm of ethics.

But this is where the struggle over form takes place—in contested terrain mapped by a shifting line between freedom and necessity. Distributing aesthetics, ethics, and economics from the humanities through the social to the natural sciences is not just an exercise for designers of college catalogues to be solved with good indexes—though a study of their location in college catalogues might prove interesting.

Because aesthetics stays on the freedom side of the line, it defies standardization and invites argument. Aesthetic judgments call for careful attention to form—the form of every argument associated with every act of judgment as well as the form of every object judged. Aesthetic practice is fluid and under constant negotiation. Unless it is abandoned altogether, as is sometimes the case with the "no accounting for taste" truism, it is necessarily conversational and social: it cannot not be free, and it cannot not be personal.

As ethics and economics drift toward the line or over it, they invite standardization and defy argument. Defying argument does not mean that they eliminate it but that they constrict its form and the area within which it can take place. In this regard, it should be noted that the aesthetic defiance of standardization also does not eliminate it but constricts its form and the area within which it can take place. At its most extreme, this constriction limits argument to descriptive dimensions, taking prescriptive dimensions off the table altogether. It makes perfect sense to argue about whether the law of gravity is best described in terms of force and attraction at a distance or in terms of the geometry of space-time, but to be a conscientious objector to that law is simply foolish and will not make it possible for you to fly.

Any shift of discussion of value toward the realm of natural science has profound implications for human freedom. If Market mechanisms are natural laws, then our economic and political behavior *vis-à-vis* those mechanisms is necessarily circumscribed in ways analogous to circumscription of our walking, climbing, and flying behavior *vis-à-vis* gravity. Descriptively, walking, climbing, and flying behavior take on highly predictable forms due to the regulating influence of gravity. Behavior that deviates widely from those forms, such as jumping off a cliff in order to fly, just does not work. This is species-specific, and it assumes no modifications. Implications for a bird jumping off a cliff are not the same as for a human, nor are implications the same for a human with a hang glider or a bungee cord. Is the same true of economic, social, and political behavior?

In responding to that question, we will come back to the discussion of law or rule as well as the discussions of form and relationship. For now, however, a few comments about the question as it relates to understanding of value will have to suffice.

3. Orientation

One of the oldest systematic discussions of value that is still readily accessible, the first book of Aristotle's *Nicomachean Ethics* (written in the fourth century BCE), begins with a formal statement that was already a commonplace at the time Aristotle wrote: the good is that at which all things aim. This leaves the content of good entirely open while offering considerable insight into the form of its relationship with things. Simply put, the commonplace claims that things are turned. This suggests that one can look at a thing and, by identifying its orientation, derive useful information about that toward which it is oriented. The challenge is to devise methods and tools by which to identify orientation, then orient one's observation accordingly. The implication is that if you are properly turned you cannot help seeing what is right in front of your eyes, an implication that does not differ greatly from Kant's and has much in common with the economic shift of value discussion toward natural science.

Adam Smith's *Wealth of Nations* (1776) is a snapshot of that shift at its eighteenth-century point of origin. Smith (a professor not of Economics but of Moral Philosophy) took up the relationship between a thing's orientation and the good toward which it is oriented in his identification of value with utility and exchange: a thing is valuable because it is useful; and because it is useful, it is in demand. Because it is in demand, it can be exchanged in a system of economic, political, and social relationships.

Smith did not write in a vacuum, and, though he is sometimes described as Capitalism's father, he is probably closer to being its midwife. In addition to utility and exchange, Smith took up his predecessors' interest in labor, Nature, and social structure. Oriented things are products of labor whose value derives from the transformation of Nature by work. Work turns Nature, and the result is exchanged in a system where maximum efficiency depends on division of labor and standardized media of exchange.

As Karl Marx noted in the following century, division of labor and standardized media of exchange have profound implications for the form of human work. Standardized media facilitate not only efficiency but also accumulation, and division of labor invites alienation. The focus can shift from work as a process in which human beings are related to Nature to the products of work which are accumulated and exchanged (not necessarily by the worker who produced them). Marx's concern with the fetishism of commodities directs our attention to a potential for confusion in which exchange value takes precedence over both human work and the utility of its products. Though the utility of an exchange value is strictly derivative, the exchange value may come to be treated as an end in itself.

Given their subsequent identification with two warring camps, there is a surprisingly large area of agreement between Marx and Smith. Most important for our purposes is the insistence that discussion of value involves attention to product, process, and producer as well as to the contexts within which they operate. Isolating any one element results in a distortion of all the others, as does forgetting that all the elements are moments in an ongoing process.

Aristotle passes on the commonplace that the good is that at which all things aim. While different things appear indisputably to aim at different things, that they aim has appeared less disputable. It is not surprising, then, that discussion of value has traditionally attended to aim and aimer as well as target.

Keeping Marx and political economy in mind, we can divide ethical theory into two broad categories, teleological and deontological, the first of which focuses on end or target (*telos*), the second of which focuses on duty or aim (*deontos*). Each of these categories can be further divided into two subcategories. Teleological theories may be utilitarian or hedonistic. Deontological theories may be primarily concerned with act or with rule. Hedonistic theories focus on particular ends and prescribe that one act in every instance so as to maximize pleasure and minimize pain. Utilitarian theories move toward a more social calculus of ends and prescribe that one act in such a way as to ensure the greatest good for the greatest number. Act deontological theories focus on particular actions but may use them to build up more general descriptive rules. Rule deontological theories focus on general rules and judge particular acts against them, usually proceeding on the assumption that the rules precede the acts.

These theories may be either descriptive or prescriptive; but, more properly, they are a combination of both. They describe the way people do act and prescribe the way we should act. To the extent that value discussion is shifted into the realm of natural science, description and prescription collapse: it is not necessary to admonish people to obey the law of gravity. Nor is it necessary, many economists since Adam Smith would tell us, to admonish people to make purchasing and investment decisions on the basis of self-interest. Prescriptive language is superfluous where natural law is concerned, not because prescription has disappeared but because it has become absolute: it goes without saying. That the territory of necessity is contested terrain is best evidenced, continuing with the purchasing and investment example, by the tendency to describe action that does not appear to be made on the basis of self-interest as irrational.

The large body of legal material associated with corporate struggles over social investing is interesting in this regard. "Fiduciary responsibility" has been defined with reference to the so-called "prudent man" standard as requiring corporate boards to invest in ways that maximize shareholder return. The rational agent, then, is one whose action is entirely determined. Because information is imperfect and incomplete, one can debate how best to maximize return; but one cannot debate whether some other basis for action is legitimate.

This is rich terrain to which we will return in subsequent chapters, but it is important to note from the outset that value circulates in ways that incline toward self-reproduction. If human labor transforms nature by using it, then the material available in nature and the physical capacities of human beings will constrain the types of labor that are likely to occur. These types will be further constrained if labor is divided for the sake of efficiency and if bits of transformed nature are exchanged or accumulated. Those who accumulate can avoid labor, and those whose labor is divided will be increasingly dependent on the accumulation of others. The kinds of work people do will be determined as much by conditions of exchange as by what they need.

The point is to say once more that conversation about value turns quickly to the relationship between freedom and necessity. If freedom disappears from the conversation, so does the matter of ethics and aesthetics. To return to the distribution of conversation about value from humanities through social to natural science, I would encourage a distribution that permeates every conversation. There are not separate aesthetic, ethical, and economic values so much as aesthetic, ethical, and economic dimensions of every value. In this case, walking backwards may require second guessing the rationality of necessary actions motivated by self-interest. The tools are ready at hand: while necessary actions of economic agents circulate in ways that constrain social relationships and human freedom, free actions of aesthetic and ethical agents may shatter the necessity in ways that transform constraints.

Two

A LABOR THEORY OF VALUE

Neither Adam Smith (1723-1790) nor Karl Marx (1818-1883) is accorded an entirely secure place in every history of philosophy, but both are indisputably significant for more broadly conceived histories of ideas, and both undoubtedly contributed to philosophical conversation in the nineteenth and twentieth centuries. They have come to represent two extremes of a conversational continuum that emerges alongside the Industrial Revolution in Great Britain. Though neither was English, both latched onto England's experience as a territory within which to explore value in the context of emerging industrial Capitalism—Smith near the beginning of its emergence, Marx after the process was already well under way.

Smith is among the early theorists of political economy which, as the label implies, combined a concern with *polis* (city), *oikos* (house), and *nomos* (law). When Smith and Marx speak of "value," both attempt to do so in ways that attend to laws by which lives are necessarily shaped at both local "household" levels and at the more global level of the cities we imagine and within which we live. Marx's writing emerged out of a background that was Hegelian (to which I will return later) but also intimately acquainted with revolutionary politics in Germany and France. Smith's writing emerged out of a background that was Humeian (to which I will also return) but at the same time intimately acquainted with the beginning of industrialization, particularly in the north of Britain. In the century following Smith, during which Marx wrote, "north" came to symbolize the new industrial Capitalist order as contrasted with the old agrarian and aristocratic order of the "south," not only in the emerging literature of political economy but also in popular fictional accounts such as those of Elizabeth Gaskell and Elizabeth Barrett Browning.

Smith draws on a distinctly Scottish empiricist tradition associated with David Hume (1711-1776) while replacing the "conscience" demanded by Hume's critics in his theory of moral sentiments with an imaginary impartial spectator only one step removed from the invisible hand to which he would later famously attribute the working of the Market. Marx draws on a distinctly German idealist tradition associated with G.W.F. Hegel (1770-1831) but seeks to right Hegel by turning to early Greek materialist and seventeenth-century British empiricist traditions. Both are pragmatic (concerned with action), both are materialist, and both are realist (not content with ideas alone), intent on turning from mere interpretation (which Marx particularly identified with philosophy) to science (which both writers, as products of the centuries within which they wrote, identified with Isaac Newton, 1642-1726). As suggested earlier, the "scientific" turn meant a turn to "necessity" as embodied in "natural" law. Newton represented that turn for the eighteenth and nineteenth centuries, though its roots lie deeper, at least a generation earlier, in Francis Bacon (1561-1626).

As noted in the first chapter, both Smith and Marx distinguish between value in use and value in exchange. In Marx's reading, one is natural, the other conventional. This distinction between natural and conventional is of critical importance for thinking about ethics. Marx argues that the proper relationship is a movement from natural to conventional. Establishing what is natural, however, is often a matter of controversy; and it is on this controversy that conversation about value, nature, and convention often turns.

Smith moves quickly in *Wealth of Nations* from the distinction between use and exchange to a pithy statement of the labor theory of value and a closely related price theory at the beginning of Chapter V:

> The value of any commodity...is equal to the quantity of labor which it enables [its owner] to purchase or command. Labor, therefore, is the real measure of the exchangeable value of all commodities. The real price of everything, what everything really costs to the man who wants to acquire it, is the toil and trouble of acquiring it. What everything is really worth to the man who has acquired it, and who wants to dispose of it or exchange it for something else, is the toil and trouble which it can save to himself, and which it can impose upon other people.

Marx and Smith agree on the importance of exchange for value, but Marx is critical of Smith's emphasis on acquisition and the effect that emphasis has on his understanding of human being. As Smith reads value, it is a measure of the labor necessary to acquire a thing. This effectively detaches both labor and value from production. For Marx, production is fundamental to being human: the human is not being so much as becoming. This is most evident in his analyses of objectification and alienation, both of which are important contributions to the theoretical understanding of value.

1. Alienation and Objectification

In Marx's analysis, labor is alienated when it is not only external but also forced, a means to an external end rather than the satisfaction of an internal need. Labor is an essential dimension of our humanity, but, when it is alienated, it is experienced as accidental. It belongs to someone else, and it is imposed from outside. That it is imposed means that it is not experienced as free; and it means that freedom is experienced—if it is experienced at all—as separate from the essentially human activity of labor (Marx, 1964, pp. 106-119; pp. 120-127).

Alienation is a distortion of objectification, the process by which a person's relation to self becomes actual through relations with others. Objectification is construction of objects, including self and world. Through labor, the laborer creates his or her relationship to the product of labor, his or her relationship to the act of production, and the relationship in which other persons stand to him or her and to his or her product. Objectification transforms nature into culture and constructs value.

As a distortion of the process by which nature is transformed into usable objects, alienation is closely related to the confusion of exchange value and use value that Marx calls "fetishism" and locates particularly in the form of commodities (Marx, 1967, pp. 71-83). At first glance, the commodity appears simple. A closer examination reveals a mystery that originates not in the commodity's utility or exchange but in its form. This form is a process in which the relations of producers are experienced as social relations among products. A commodity is mysterious because it hides the social character of labor behind an objective character stamped into labor's product.

Useful things become commodities because they are products of isolated individuals or groups. Producers do not come together until they exchange their products, so the social character of their labor shows itself only in the act of exchange. The social dimension of labor, then, appears to be a result of the relation which the act of exchange establishes among labor's products. Exchange value, experienced as a natural characteristic of products, is a convention, a social product, fixed through interaction of products as quantities of value. Use value is not a natural attribute of the object but a natural outcome of labor: it is intrinsic to the process of labor itself.

Marx highlights a two-fold inversion in which exchange among isolated producers becomes primary while the utility of social products becomes secondary. Inverting this inversion would result in a natural state of affairs: the social character of labor and the utility of social products would be primary, while separate selves and systems of exchange would be secondary. The point is not to render one end of the process less real than the other, but to clarify relationships among product, process, and producer. Here again, walking backwards may help us get a better look at the play.

Marx maintains that a structure (such as value) is best understood as an equilibrated state of an ongoing process. It is product of the process that has preceded it, basis of the process proceeding through it to its transformations (which are also equilibrated states), and producer of the transformations that follow it.

2. Symbols and Signs

In *Play, Dreams, and Imitation in Childhood*, Jean Piaget (1896-1980) draws on Sassurrean linguistics to distinguish the sign, in which the relationship between signifier and signified is arbitrary or conventional, from the symbol, in which the signifier bears a resemblance of some kind to the thing signified (Piaget, 1962, p. 169). The distinction is a useful one for discussion of value. Value in use, like Piaget's symbol, is motivated. A symbol resembles the thing symbolized, and an object of utility is used. No social convention is required to designate the symbol as symbol or the object of utility as valuable. Value in exchange, like Piaget's sign, is conventional: it is a social product. Systems of exchange value, like the systems of signs that constitute language, are not motivated: a social convention is required to designate the sign as sign or the object of exchange as value.

That at least one aspect of value is associated with convention has important implications for the experience of freedom in action, some of which may be illuminated with reference to imperatives. An imperative is something that one must do, which seems to place it beyond "ought," beyond the realm of freedom. To say, for example, that you must eat and breathe is to express a necessity rather than to propose a freely chosen act. In the United States, one might also say that you must drive on the right side of the road. In each case, there is an assumed conclusion: one must eat and breathe in order to go on living. One must drive on the right side of the road in order to avoid a collision. There is, however, an obvious and important difference between the two cases. The first case is natural, the second conventional. This does not make the second any less real, but it does embed it in a set of social conventions, a set that would change, for example, if you were driving in England or Zimbabwe instead of the United States.

What if we said that you must eat with a fork or that you must eat three meals a day? Though we still use the language of necessity, its import has changed. A less trivial example arises in the routine deployment of imperatives in war time, as in "you must bomb this or that target" or "you must register for the draft when you turn eighteen." A person who confuses a conventional imperative such as "you must eat with a fork" and a biological imperative such as "you must eat" is a candidate for psychiatric care. Not eating with a fork is generally not life threatening, and it is even polite in some contexts—when dining in an Ethiopian restaurant, for example, or when presented with chopsticks and a Chinese entree. But what of the bombing imperative? What is the connection between custom or convention and moral judgment?

Strictly speaking, a biological imperative such as eating is not a matter of judgment at all—unless one is contemplating a hunger strike or suicide by starvation. The same might be said of custom. Driving on the left side of the road in the United States as a matter of principle would not only be odd but also dangerous. Eating with your hands would in most cases be considered rude but innocuous. But the bombing question is another matter.

Bombing is more than rude, and disobeying an order may be considered treasonous. Neither is innocuous. We need a way to distinguish between imperatives that are strictly conventional and those that are moral, because imperatives, like commodities, may be fetishized. The two are distinguished at least by the fact that a conventional imperative is culture specific, while a moral imperative is not. Paradoxically, this imparts a degree of necessity to moral imperatives that appears to diminish the realm of freedom and relegate the matter of ethics to convention. I will return to this paradox in the discussion of confession in the final two chapters of the book.

How is the biological imperative "you must eat" transformed when it is spoken, for example, at the bedside of a terminally ill loved one nauseous from chemotherapy, who is neither hungry nor terribly interested at that moment in living? It may be that Kant misplaced the matter of ethics, which is not so much freedom as the intersection of freedom with necessity. The question is what lies at that intersection. Jean Piaget's use of the relationship between logical necessity and possibility (if not-p is possible, p is not necessary; if not-p is necessary, p is not possible) as a basis for his understanding of play is instructive: play is a process by which possibility is cultivated in a field of necessity. Is there an analogous process in ethics?

A conventional imperative may appear to be a moral one. This can reduce ethics to a discipline that describes acceptable behaviors within a given social context. Under such circumstances, ethics becomes a branch of decision theory with an essentially conservative function in society. Another function of ethics, however, is to expose the confusion of moral and conventional imperatives. It is this function that makes the movement from description to prescription possible.

Just as Marx described alienation and fetishism in terms of inversion, where what is natural comes to be seen as conventional and what is conventional comes to be seen as natural, we can describe moral alienation and fetishism, where what is conventional comes to be seen as morally imperative and what is morally imperative comes to be seen as conventional. In each case, movement from description to prescription requires generation of possibility out of necessity's appearance.

3. Possibility and Play

Generation of possibility requires what Jerome Bruner calls subjunctive thinking, a type of play. Piaget recognized the importance of play for epistemology. I am convinced that it has a central role in ethics as well, not because, as Maria

Montessori said, play is the child's work, but because play and work together are indispensable dimensions of the construction of human worlds. This construction of human worlds in the interplay of necessity and freedom associated with work and play is critical, and I will return to it more than once in later chapters. For now, a brief outline of Piaget's theory will suffice.

Piaget, like Marx and Smith, contributed to the direction of philosophical conversation about value by exploring territory outside the realm of philosophy. I suggested earlier that Smith in the eighteenth century, then Marx in the nineteenth, took up a seventeenth-century advance in physics identified with Newton. One side effect of this appropriation was a tendency toward determinism that certainly complicated discussion of freedom. Piaget advances the conversation by attending to a nineteenth-century development in biology and—to a lesser extent—a development in physics that occurred just at the beginning of the twentieth century. The biological development is evolutionary theory, systematized and articulated in the middle of the nineteenth century by Charles Darwin (1809-1882). It is not surprising that Piaget took this up, since his graduate study was in biology and philosophy. His development of the theory is particularly important, though, because it is quite distinct from the "social" Darwinism associated with Herbert Spencer (1820-1903) and the quasi-biological determinism characteristic of Sigmund Freud (1856-1939). Freud and Spencer both had an enormous—and often negative—impact on followers of Marx and Smith, so Piaget's alternative track holds particular promise. The development in physics is relativity theory, articulated by Albert Einstein (1879-1955) in a series of papers published in 1905. Piaget responds explicitly to this theory in important studies of space, time, and number that he conducted during the course of his long and productive career. Detailed exploration of those studies would divert our attention from the conversation about value that is our primary concern here. Suffice it to say that Einstein's work, together with the epistemological turn that Piaget took with many post-Kantian philosophers under the influence not only of Kant but also of the British empiricists who inspired Kant's concern with the limits of human understanding, resulted in a clear repudiation of simple determinism—biological or otherwise—in favor of what Piaget called genetic epistemology or, more generally and more simply, constructivism.

Construction (making) and practice (doing) are central to Piaget's description of the equilibration of cognitive structures. Structures (including the self, objects, and worlds) are not static things but aspects of dynamic constructive processes analogous to organic growth, which consists of activity directed toward equilibrium. That structures are processes directs our attention to equilibration rather than equilibria understood as finished states (Piaget, 1985). This is not to ignore states, but to see them within the context of processes of which they are parts and to recognize that they are not finished. Piaget's theory of knowledge is not primarily a theory of equilibrium or a hierarchical ordering of equilibria (and therefore not primarily a stage theory) but a theory of equilibration, a constructive process rather than a particular end or collection of ends (Turner, 1973). Activity directed toward equilibrium proceeds by means of two functionally invariant processes, assimilation ("incorporation of an external element...into a sensory-motor or conceptual scheme of the subject") and accommodation (modification of such schemes by the influence of the environment). The equilibration of cognitive structures is a subcategory of the evolutionary process of adaptation, which, as Piaget understands it, is not a process of conforming to a preformed external environment but a process in which both organism and environment are constructed and transformed (Piaget, 1971; 1980; 1985, pp. 5-6).

Assimilation and accommodation always proceed together, though assimilation predominates at first. Piaget's "equilibration" is an interplay of these processes that reflects "different relationships between the subject and objects or between the subject's schemes" all of which "share a common form in their structural mechanism—all require increasingly complete and detailed compensations between positive properties or affirmations and the corresponding negations." This means that development may also be described as a movement from "primacy of affirmations or positive characteristics" toward "reversibility," and it makes reversible operations, or cooperation, central to adaptation while reflecting Piaget's emphasis on "optimizing equilibration" (Piaget, 1971, pp. 143-144).

Piaget speaks of optimizing equilibration with two reservations: it must not be "reduced to a march toward static equilibrium" and it must not be "conceived in terms of a pure evolutionism leading into a radical becoming that forgets the mechanisms of transmission and the fact that every improvement is oriented in the direction of coherence or more developed forms of internal necessity." With these reservations, Piaget sought to avoid the two tyrannies of geneticism and environmentalism. They allow his theory to incorporate necessity without becoming either biologically or environmentally deterministic (Piaget, 1985, pp. 143-144).

In human development, equilibration begins as a process of decentration, a "Copernican revolution." The child progresses from grasping everything toward perception of himself or herself as one entity among others in a universe that she or he has gradually constructed and which hereafter will be experienced as external. The child moves toward cooperation, which involves the ability to dissociate his or her point of view from the points of view of others and coordinate these different points of view (Piaget, 1968). To coordinate structures is to incorporate them into more inclusive structures. To coordinate points of view is to construct a structure within which both points of view can exist. Piaget describes this movement toward cooperation as socialization of action and internalization which gives rise to thought.

Socialization represents society's internalization of the self: construction of a self is simultaneously incorporation of the self into society. Development, which progresses from activity toward concept, involves construction and transformation of a self in the context of a society that is itself constructed and transformed. At the same time, in the construction of representational thought, society is engaged in constructing the child.

Drawing on Marx's concept of work and Piaget's concept of play, I propose the following as a preliminary formulation of the construction of human worlds in the interplay of necessity and freedom: work—associated with accommodation, closure, and stability—is the process by which value is generated and reproduced, while play—associated with assimilation, openness, and instability—is the process by which value is transformed. Like assimilation and accommodation, the two are inseparable aspects of a single process of equilibration. As in Piaget's epistemology, the process becomes more and more equilibrated, balancing in this case the openness of play and possibility with the closure of work. As in Piaget's epistemology and in Marx's theory of value, the proper focus for inquiry is the process of construction and transformation itself rather than particular works that emerge along the way.

Chapter Three

THE END OF ETHICS

In the first book of his *Nicomachean Ethics*, Aristotle begins with a formal theory ("the good is that at which all things aim") and moves toward a practical method (which he calls "politics"). John Stuart Mill (1806-1873) is also interested in method, though he begins with a set of assumptions about the importance of ends. Although the form of ethical behavior may not be as obvious as Aristotle's starting point suggests, agreement on form has often proven useful as a starting point for discussion of relationships between means and ends—particularly where agreement on ends is elusive.

1. A Principle of Utility

Mill claims that utilitarianism was first articulated in the fourth century BCE by Socrates in his *Protagoras* (to which I will devote more attention later) emphasizing that all action is for the sake of some end, which recalls the "assumed conclusion" in the discussion of imperatives in the previous chapter. The structure of action is teleological, and it is in that structure that general principles of ethics are to be located. *A priori* theorists (including Kant, to whom I will also attend later) employ a "principle of utility," according to Mill, with or without acknowledgment. That principle maintains that right action increases happiness while wrong action decreases happiness, increases pain, or both.

Like Jeremy Bentham (1748-1832), Mill embeds this in a social dimension, so that the principle of utility judges an action right when it produces the greatest good for the greatest number. Mill departs from Bentham in his inclusion of quality as well as quantity as aspects of the greatest good. Unlike Bentham, Mill does not propose an ethical calculus, though he continues to define ethics in terms of decision. The task of ethics, Mill maintains, is to help us choose which option is right when we are confronted with a range of options.

Mill dismisses the existence of an innate moral sense, arguing that moral feelings are acquired. In this, he is virtually a mirror image of Kant. He inherits the empiricism of John Locke (1632-1704) via Hume, but he confronts rationalism. He also confronts the "common sense realism" of Thomas Reid (1710-1796), who succeeded Adam Smith at Glasgow. Reid was a critic of empiricism who held that moral first principles are self-evident objects of moral intuition and distinguished sensation, an act of mind with no object distinct from the act, from perception, which is related to other objects and is immediate, not the result of reasoning. Part of Mill's inheritance is an associationism that accounts for the emergence of moral sense out of moral experience. Without making too fine a point here of Mill's response to Reid's distinction between sensation and perception, it is worth noting that Mill articulates an empiricist position to the extent that moral sensation and perception are necessarily connected with moral experience. This is pragmaticist as much as empiricist, grounding sensation and perception in action. As Piaget would also note later, armed with evolutionary theory (particularly in its Francophone form), that moral sense is constructed in action does not mean that it is not natural.

Locke's empiricism, outlined in his inquiry into knowledge and belief, is an indispensable background for Mill. According to Locke, ideas cannot be innate, because they are invariably outcomes of experience derived either from internal sources (processes of our minds) or external sources (sensibly perceived). Sensation conveys information about external objects, while reflection conveys information about internal processes. Ideas may be simple or complex. Human power consists in compounding and dividing simple ideas, the basic building blocks of thought. These basic building blocks are grouped into four divisions:

- those which come into our minds by one sense only,
- those which come into our minds by more than one sense,
- those which are had "from reflection only," and
- those which make their way into the mind "by all the ways of sensation and reflection."

Mind engages in two principle actions, perception or thinking and volition or willing. As complex objects in mind, ideas are analogous to qualities in body. Qualities may be primary (designated by such terms of sensation as bulk, figure, number, situation, motion or rest), or they may be powers (having the ability to change other bodies, causing them to act on our senses in different ways.) The idea is no more a likeness of the thing it represents than is a name the likeness of the thing it names. Knowledge progresses from perception, an act of thinking, through retention to discernment, both acts of willing, as mind exerts its power over simple ideas in one of three ways:

- by combining simple ideas into compounds, thus creating complex ideas;
- by bringing two simple or complex ideas together to view them at the same time, thus creating ideas of relations; and
- by separating them from other ideas that accompany them in real existence, thus abstracting them and creating general ideas.

Because Locke's mind, in spite of his association with the infamous *tabula rasa*, is a place of perceptual activity more than a passive receptacle, it is the point at which human beings and our worlds intersect, and that makes it the place of liberty, which Locke identifies as "a power in any agent to do or forbear any particular action, according to the determination or thought of the mind, whereby either of them is preferred to the other." If either doing or not doing an action "is not in the power of the agent," she or he is under necessity, not at liberty. The voluntary is opposed to the involuntary, not to the necessary. Freedom "consists in the dependence of the existence, or nonexistence of any *action*, upon our *volition* of it; and not in the dependence of any action, or its contrary, on our *preference*."

Note again the relationship between necessity and possibility. Where there is no possibility of action or inaction, the matter of ethics evaporates. However, if action is teleological, there must be a necessary connection between an act and its end. Necessary consequences give free actions their imperative quality.

Hume's skepticism radicalized Locke's empiricism by calling the possibility of necessary connections into question. What we call causation is nothing but a temporal artifact. We can observe one thing following another, but we cannot establish that the second was caused by the first. If two events are temporally or spatially proximate, we may connect them mentally, but they are not necessarily connected outside our minds. Hume replaces an orderly world structured by necessary causal connections with a field of accidents structured by nothing more than chance. Custom takes the place of necessity.

Mill, like Kant, reacts to this corrosive skepticism in the form articulated by Hume. But both are aware, as we should be, that it was present in some of the earliest empirical speculation to which we have access, that of early atomists such as Democritus (460-360 BCE) and Leucippus (490-430 BCE), to which both Plato (428-348 BCE) and Aristotle (384-322 BCE) responded. Mill and Kant revisit earlier questions when they ask what is left after relentless analysis has been applied to every possibility. For Mill, what is left is not only law but also action. This is promising, because it introduces the possibility that such an "after" is itself not a possibility. To understand self, other, and law, it is necessary to examine the structure of action itself. In this, Mill is largely in agreement with Kant. Law (*nomos*) joins their ethical accounts by means of action in narrative and character.

2. Silence

I have already hinted that what is often referred to as the epistemological turn of post-Kantian philosophy might just as well be characterized as a continuation of the conversation about the limits of human understanding associated with the empiricism of Locke, Berkeley, and Hume. Kant certainly saw himself as part of this conversation, and one advantage of this characterization is that it avoids a potentially disastrous heroic segmentation of the history of ideas. Kant drew on British empiricism and continental rationalism in ways that influenced Hegelian idealism. Two of the most important thinkers of the nineteenth century, Marx and Søren Kierkegaard (1813-1855), neither entirely comfortable in the category of "philosopher," wrote largely in reaction to Hegel, against abstract system as much as against idealism. Mill did not write in reaction to Hegel, and this may have helped him avoid simply conflating his inherited empiricism with materialism, a conflation toward which Marx was inclined after his move to London in 1849. It is interesting that Kierkegaard's reaction to Hegel, developed at roughly the same time Marx and Mill were writing, took up a concern with the person that Mill shared and that he identified in an often overlooked Coleridgean strand of British thought. I have considered that strand in detail elsewhere (Schroeder, 1999), so I focus here on consideration of Kierkegaard's confrontation with abstract system. Given Hegel's fascination with universals and the tendency toward determinism already noted in the competing systems of thought that developed out of Marx and Smith, it is significant that Kierkegaard attended carefully to the question of how silence and speech emerge out of the encounter between particular and universal—and how ethics is related to both.

In *Fear and Trembling*, Kierkegaard directly addresses the end of ethics when he asks, "Was Abraham ethically defensible in keeping silent about his purpose before Sarah, before Eleazar, before Isaac?" The ethical, he writes, is the "universal." As the universal, it is manifest, revealed. The individual, on the other hand, is hidden, concealed" (p. 91). The ethical task of the individual is "to develop out of this concealment" and reveal himself or herself "in the universal." Here, Kierkegaard explicitly connects ethics with story: the ethical task is to communicate. Whenever the individual "wills to remain in concealment," she or he sins and lies in temptation (*Anfechtung*). She or he can come out of this only by revealing himself or herself, hence only by speaking. "If there is not a concealment which has its ground in the fact that the individual as the individual is higher than the universal," Kierkegaard writes, "then Abraham's conduct is indefensible, for he paid no heed to the intermediate ethical determinants." If there is such a concealment, we are in the presence of a paradox (p. 92).

Kierkegaard marks an aesthetic category, the interesting, as "the category of the turning-point," especially important to an age that lives in a turning-point in history—and is there any age that does not? The "interesting" is a border-category between aesthetics and ethics (p. 93). Kierkegaard cites Aristotle's distinction between two parts of myth: change (*peripeteia*) and recognition (*anagnorisis*). Where there can be a question of recognition, it goes without saying that there has been a concealment. Concealment is the factor of tension in drama, just as recognition is the relaxing factor. Fate is crucial to the working of Greek tragedy, which Kierkegaard calls blind. Modern drama, on the other hand, makes everything dependent on the free act of the hero. Kierkegaard argues for a diminished emphasis on will, an enhancement of fate or chance. We will return to this.

Kierkegaard insists that it is necessary "to show the absolute difference between the aesthetic concealment and the paradox" (p. 94). The tragic hero, the favorite of ethics, is

> the purely human, and him I can understand, and all he does is in the light of the revealed. If I go further, then I stumble upon the paradox, either the divine or the demoniac, for silence is both. Silence is the snare of the demon, and the more one keeps silent, the more terrifying the demon becomes; but silence is also the mutual understanding between the Deity and the individual. (p. 97)

The reason for Abraham's silence "is not that he as the individual would place himself in an absolute relation to the universal, but that he as the individual was placed in an absolute relation to the absolute" (p. 103). Two important distinctions are employed here: that between the universal and the absolute, and that between the individual placing himself or herself and the individual being placed. Kierkegaard insists on an element of givenness that precedes free acts. Faith, as passion, precedes freedom.

The genuine tragic hero

> sacrifices himself and all that is his for the universal, his deed and every emotion with him belong to the universal, he is revealed, and in this self-revelation he is the beloved son of ethics. This does not fit the case of Abraham: he does nothing for the universal, and he is concealed.... Now we reach the paradox. Either the individual as the individual is able to stand in an absolute relation to the absolute (and then the ethical is not the highest)/or Abraham is lost—he is neither a tragic hero nor an aesthetic hero. (Kierkegaard, p. 122)

Abraham's distress lies in the fact that he cannot speak intelligibly and is thus effectively silenced. His words to Isaac, that God will provide, are evidence of his double movement. If he had only renounced Isaac, these words would be a lie. Because he has not only renounced but also made the movement of faith, they are not untrue. On the other hand, they say nothing, because they are spoken in a language so foreign that it is necessarily incomprehensible (Kierkegaard, p. 128).

3. Activity, State, and Habit

As I have repeatedly emphasized, the conversation is an old one. Much of the groundwork is laid between Plato and Aristotle. Kierkegaard's relentlessly practical concern with action in a social context that may simultaneously demand word—whether in the form of speech or in the form of silence—develops against the background of Aristotle's argument with Plato over the interrelationship of soul and character with action in the world.

The definition of good with which Aristotle begins his *Nicomachean Ethics* is distinguished both by its common character—it has the form of a truism—and by its purely formal character. To make the definition concrete, he shifts from language about good to language about particular goods, from a formal definition of good as *telos* to the particularity of human good, which he understands to be happiness. Happiness is defined as an activity of soul in accordance with virtue, and virtue is defined as a state of character.

Happiness is an activity, virtue is a state, and character is the unifying factor between them. Aristotle connects character with habit (*hexis*). Both are acquired by acting. A habit predisposes toward particular decisions, either good or bad, in particular situations and thus may be described as either a virtue or a vice. These particular states, together with the process of which they are a part, constitute what Aristotle identifies as character. Character is what makes it possible to attribute action to a person, to "explain ourselves" as Lewis Carroll's caterpillar demanded.

In Aristotle's account, this is closely related to the concept of soul. The soul is that which makes a thing what it is. Character is that which makes a person who she or he is. Soul is associated with nature or essence, while character is associated with structure and identity.

As structure of action, character is uniquely human. In Aristotle's account, this structure is not only related to essence and process but also to the substructures he identifies as virtues. Particular virtues constitute substructures within the inclusive structure of character. Virtue as such is more generally associated with a structure of character described as a disposition to choose a mean that lies between extremes identified as vices. It is this disposition that makes it possible for the mean to be grasped by perception rather than by reasoning. Virtue is a disposition to do the right thing. It is a function of perception because "the right thing" has to be recognized in context. Aristotle's virtue involves an ability to look at parts and see the whole, to act in particular cases in a way that is conscious of the whole. It is important to emphasize that the mean is not some sort of compromise that lies between opposites, certainly not an amalgam of "good" and "evil." It is more properly a vehicle by which Aristotle insists on the perceptual imperative to see into the heart of things.

Virtue is associated not with compromise but with a small target surrounded by a sea of vice.

Alasdair MacIntyre reads Aristotle against the background of the heroic society depicted in Homer's *Iliad*, where morality and social structure are identical. Agonizing over distinctions between custom and moral imperative makes no sense in this society, where to be moral is to play one's role and not to play one's role is to be immoral. This equation of morality with social structure connects morality with story as surely as Kierkegaard's discussion of Abraham's silence, with its Hegelian background, because human lives take the form of story and because "the self becomes what it is in heroic societies only through its role; it is a social creation, not an individual one" (MacIntyre, p. 129).

Aristotle's "character" derives from this understanding of self as story, as is made explicit in the *Poetics*. Story is what binds past, present, and future together; and character is the form story takes in human lives. Without character as story, we would not be able to identify actions as uncharacteristic—or as immoral. Society, like the self, is a story. Heroic epics—including the *Iliad*, the *Aeneid*, and the Arthurian legends—literally form society. By defining the heroic, these epics make it possible to identify roles and judge whether these roles are being filled.

In Kierkegaard's account, story is intimately connected with communication. But here Kierkegaard characteristically gives the back of his hand to Hegel, who, like earlier writers of heroic epics, thought communication was fully comprehended in speech and action. The imposition of silence is paradoxically communicative in Kierkegaard's discussion of Abraham, both in its disconnection of moral activity from preference and in its absolute isolation of the individual from an impersonal universal. In Aristotle, a structural account of story advances it as a possible alternative to the universal. Abraham's absolute relation to the absolute embeds him in a story that communicates through his silence as it undermines any external universal by which his action could be finally and simply explained. Note that such a universal would cut off communication by speaking the last word. Abraham's silence ensures that communication will stay open.

This background helps explain why Aristotle, like Plato, connects being a good person with being a good citizen and connects both with organic processes. The heroic epics identify virtue with excellence (both translate *arete*) and focus particularly on excellence in struggle. This struggle most often takes the form of war, so that the virtuous person is the excellent warrior. Aristotle, following Plato, shifted the struggle from the battlefield to the *polis*, thereby shifting attention from participation in war to participation in politics. The citizen, in this sense, is equivalent to the warrior, and the question of virtue is still a question of excellence. Aristotle and Plato, as surely as Homer, "adopt a stance on the narrative character of human life" (MacIntyre, p. 144). They tell stories that provide contexts within which to judge human action.

Chapter Four

VIRTUE IN ACTION

The earliest cosmological and cosmogonical speculation in Greek, essential to understanding the philosophical tradition that blossomed in Plato and Aristotle, is found in the work of Homer and Hesiod, dating probably from the seventh and eighth centuries BCE, though extant written versions are more recent (Kirk and Raven, 1971; Diels, 1934-1954; Freeman, 1957). Traditional accounts name Thales, who wrote in the early 6th century BCE, as the first philosopher, but the earliest of those accounts suggest either that he did not write at all or that he wrote in epic verse. Nothing survives of his work except a few citations in later authors. The fragmentary survival of the work of the whole body of philosophers known as presocratic means that the label communicates more about timing than about content. These philosophers, including Thales, predate Socrates (469-399 BCE), though the latest of the philosophers generally designated by the label, Democritus of Abdera, who was in his prime around 420 BCE, and Diogenes of Apollonia, who lived in the later half of the fifth century BCE, are his only slightly older contemporaries; beyond that, they are a decidedly diverse group. What is most revealing about the label is that it follows Plato in designating Socrates as a watershed in philosophical history. Like the birth of Jesus, the *Hijra*, and the creation of the world, Socrates is seen in the West as an event by which other events may be dated.

There is in many cases considerable controversy regarding whether particular presocratic philosophers wrote at all. Socrates, too, was suspicious of writing, including books. In the portrait passed on to us by Plato, he did not write them. To the extent that Socrates is the watershed by which Western philosophy measures itself and the world, philosophy is, at its origin, an oral discipline: Socrates, like Homer, sang divinely inspired words. Plato seems to have only reluctantly resorted to writing them down, thereby becoming a poet. His well known distrust of poets is an indication that he shared his predecessors' faith in the power of words. What made them powerful also made them dangerous. Socrates and some of his predecessors responded to this danger by avoiding the written word, preferring the more malleable and more organic spoken form. Plato responded by suggesting that poets and poetry be kept on a short leash. He was convinced of the political and educational power of a good story and seems to have been convinced that one political function of the philosopher was to properly discriminate between "good" stories and "bad" ones.

In this regard, it is important to recall that the great epics out of which the concept of Greece was born are war stories centered on a struggle with Ilium

(Troy) that transformed twelfth-century Mycenaean warlords like Agamemnon into the heroic forbears of Greek civilization. That transformation was intertwined with a centuries-long process by which the Trojan War was recast as a battle between Europe and Asia. Without the Persian threat, projected back into the Trojan threat by historians such as Herodotus (484-425 BCE), there would have been no occasion to think of Hellas at all. The pivotal role of Athenian naval power in the later struggles against the Persians made it possible for increasingly self-conscious Athenian writers to make Athens the center of Hellas at the same time that philosophical and literary activity moved from the periphery toward that Athenian center. The Athenian invention of Greece hinged on a Greek invention of Persia.

The geographic process by which Greece, then Rome, then the West were constructed in the invention of others is intimately connected to the construction of disciplines by which philosophy and then science are set apart from poetry and theology and accorded special status, and the construction of canons by which "true" stories are set apart from "false" ones. Terms such as *agrioi* (which might be translated as "rube" or "redneck") and *barbaroi* (which came to carry a force similar to its English derivative "barbarian") were extant as early as Homer in Greek literature (Mudimbe, 1993). But the social process of their definition is coterminous with the emergence of Athens as the center of Hellas and is more important than their existence at the beginning of that literature. From the beginning, they function as names, categorical distinctions that draw a line between those who live in the city and those who do not. That line is older than the Greek language, as evinced, for example, by the *Epic of Gilgamesh*, but it is instructive. Cities play a crucial role in the construction of both history and geography. In fact, histories of the West almost always begin by designating the Sumerians, the first builders of cities, as the dividing line between prehistory and history, and maps almost always begin by picturing what is not city as empty. *Agrioi* is one of several terms that function to distinguish "us" from "them," and in the Homeric universe, this has the important effect of drawing a circle that includes both Ilium and the Greek city states while it excludes those who do not live in cities. This is one reason why it is possible for Homer to paint a sympathetic picture of the Trojans even as he depicts them as engaged in life and death struggle with the Greeks. It may also be what makes the Greeks appear progressively less civilized as the time they spend outside the city is protracted by the war. *Barbaroi* draws a different circle, one that divides the Trojans from the Greeks on the basis of language. This is the beginning of a hierarchy that is of profound importance for the invention of the West. It designates those who speak "our" language and live in "our" city as most human, those who speak "our" language but live in "other" cities as less human, those who speak "other" languages and live in "other" cities as less human still, and those who live "outside" the city and speak "other" languages as little better than animals, who, it should be noted, live "outside" both the city and language, except in the case of domesticated animals which have historically complicated the hierarchy.

This process of division is thoroughly intertwined with religion. In the emergence of a Greece centered on Athens, where the most salient feature is the invention of Persia as "other," it is instructive that two famous trials of philosophers, that of Anaxagoras (500-428 BCE) and that of Socrates, hinged on the charge of impiety. In the case of Anaxagoras, one source expands "impiety" by suggesting that the accusation was "impiety and Medism." To the extent that "Medism" designates Persian influence, it evidently had been present from before the time of Thales, but it seems to have become a problem in the peculiar construction of Greece that defined Athens at the time of the Peloponnesian War. That is to say that, whether the charges against Socrates and Anaxagoras were trumped up or not, "Athenocentrism" had become the standard by which "true" stories were distinguished from "false" ones: anything that threatened Athenian hegemony was, by definition, impious.

Plato's ambivalent relation to this development is reflected in his distrust of poets and his defense of Socrates. He seems not to have disputed the Athenocentric construction of history, though his Spartan sympathies and his brief experiment with politics in Syracuse suggest that he blamed Athenian democracy for the disintegration of Greece, which is practically indistinguishable from the execution of Socrates in his account. For Plato, as we will see later in discussion of the *Republic*, the only legitimate act of *poiēsis* is the construction of the true city: the poem that constructs a true city is a true story; all others are false.

Before examining the *Republic* and the construction of true cities in detail, I turn to another of Plato's dialogues, *Protagoras*, which begins with the question of whether virtue can be taught. That question leads to discussion of the meaning of virtue itself. More importantly, the discussion itself displays virtue in action by constructing the character of Socrates. The discussion of virtue and the construction of the particular character of Socrates serve as indispensable background for city building.

1. Two Arts

Protagoras was written toward the end of the period of Plato's earlier dialogues (398-388 BCE). The meeting between Socrates and Protagoras described in the dialogue is set at the end of the peace that followed the Persian War, about 435 BCE—before the Peloponnesian War, which lasted from 431-404 BCE. Protagoras would have been near sixty years old, Socrates in his thirties.

At the time in which the dialogue is set, we have every reason to believe that the atmosphere of Athens was generally confident, but there was also good reason in the global context for growing anxiety. Plato, with the benefit of hindsight, was acutely aware of both the confidence and the anxiety. Describing the period in *The Fragility of Goodness*, Martha Nussbaum draws on the contrast between *tuchē* (luck or "what just happens") and *technē* (human art or science). For Plato, she notes, a primary task of philosophical art is elimination or control of human exposure to luck. It is, therefore, plausible to join Nussbaum in reading the dialogue as a competition between two figures, each of whom represents a distinct *technē*, an art or science that addresses problems posed by human exposure to luck (p. 90).

As the dialogue opens, Hippocrates expresses his desire to lead Socrates to Protagoras—or, more properly as it turns out, to be led to Protagoras by Socrates. Socrates tests the strength of his resolution by probing what exactly he will be paying for if he pays Protagoras to teach him. If he paid a physician, he would become a physician. If he paid a sculptor, he would become a sculptor. Does this mean, Socrates wonders, that he is to pay Protagoras to make him a Sophist?

When this question is put to Protagoras himself, he claims to teach the art of politics, promising to make his students good citizens (318a-319a). Not only is it possible to teach virtue, Protagoras confidently maintains, he actually teaches it with regularity. Socrates is doubtful, illustrating with examples of good persons who have not succeeded in making others good (319e-320b). Protagoras calls up a myth to put Socrates's mind at ease.

Socrates and Protagoras both deploy narrative with regularity in their conversation. Both use stories to clarify and to communicate. More specifically, both use myth, drawing on a common store that would be familiar to their audience, the same common store that was the stuff of tragedies.

Protagoras's myth is a variation on an old story in which distribution of proper qualities to animals, including human beings, was delegated by Zeus to Epimetheus. He carefully distributed natural means of protection and other useful things to all the animals without realizing that he had distributed everything available before he got to humankind. His brother Prometheus came to humanity's rescue by stealing the mechanical arts of Hephaestus and Athena, as well as fire, giving them to human beings and suffering the consequences— which included being chained to a rock and having his liver eternally consumed by vultures. He could not, however, steal the art of politics, which belonged to Zeus. When human beings began to build cities, they were well on their way to being destroyed and dispersed, because they had no political arts. Zeus, fearing they would completely destroy themselves, sent Hermes with justice and reverence as ordering principles for cities and other communities. Hermes asked how he should distribute them—like the arts, to a select few only, or to everyone equally. Zeus ordered that they be given to everyone and that anyone who did not possess them should be put to death, because cities could not exist if only a few shared virtue as only a few possess the arts.

Nussbaum reads the story as a progression that begins with proto-humans wandering over the earth unable to make themselves safe. They would have died had Prometheus not given them *technai*—arts they needed to protect themselves from exposure to *tuchē*. Though this made them safer, *tuchē* remained, and humans were still prone to passion; so the story of the gift of *technai* marked a partial victory over contingency that promised something more. The story is "an account of gradually increasing human control over contingency," an early version of the myth of progress (Nussbaum, pp. 90-91).

After Protagoras finishes his long speech, Socrates comments drily that he does not generally trust either books or people who make long speeches, because neither can answer when one has a question to ask—present company excluded, of course. Protagoras can not only make long speeches but also listen to, ask, and respond to questions. So Socrates asks one: "is virtue one whole of which justice, temperance, and holiness are parts; or are all of these different names for the same thing?" Without hesitating, Protagoras answers that these qualities are parts of virtue, which is itself a whole. This leads to a further question: in what sense are they parts? Are they like mouth, nose, eyes, and ears—which are parts of the face, or are they like parts (that is, pieces) of gold—which differ from one another and from the whole only in terms of size? Protagoras again responds quickly: they are like the parts of the face (328e-330b).

Socrates then leads Protagoras to claim that a person may have some parts of virtue without necessarily having an equal share of all parts. Justice and holiness, he maintains, are discrete things. Justice is just. Holiness is holy. But the parts of virtue are not alike. So justice is not holy, and holiness is not just. By exposing the absurd consequences of these sharp distinctions among supposedly discrete parts of virtue, Socrates pushes Protagoras to admit that the parts of virtue he has enumerated are really one and the same.

Parallel to the discussion of virtue and its supposed parts is a methodological demonstration, part of the contest Nussbaum describes. Socrates insists on dialogue, while Protagoras resists (334c-338e). This is a clue to the structure and direction of Plato's work. Is it an answer one seeks—whether from Socrates or Protagoras—or is it a way of posing and exploring a problem? Protagoras quotes Simonides: "Hardly on the one hand can a man become truly good, built four-square in hands and feet and mind, a work without a flaw," (339b) then cites a second passage that he says contradicts the first: "I do not agree with the word of Pittacus, albeit the utterance of a wise man: hardly can a man be good" (339c-339d). He wants Socrates to acknowledge that the poem is a good and true composition which nevertheless contains a contradiction. Socrates, however, maintains that the two statements are consistent. This is so because being and becoming are not the same. Simonides's point, Socrates maintains, is that the truly hard thing is not to be good, but to become good (340c). This capsulizes the method Plato advances in this dialogue: emphasis on becoming as opposed to being, coupled with the insistence that good and true compositions do not contain contradictions. I will return to this in further discussion of Nussbaum and in discussion of Plato's *Republic*.

Protagoras modifies his earlier insistence that the parts of virtue are different by saying that four of the five parts—righteousness, holiness, temperance, and wisdom—are "to some extent similar," while the fifth—courage—is different. His proof is that many unrighteous, unholy, intemperate, ignorant persons are "nevertheless remarkable for their courage" (349d). Not surprisingly, Socrates does not leave this argument unquestioned. The line of questioning it initiates continues to the end of the dialogue and pushes Protagoras toward the admission that one cannot be courageous without also being wise, since courage includes knowledge of what is dangerous and what is not.

In the end, Socrates brings a sullen Protagoras back around as a friendly partner in dialogue by declaring that neither has won an argument. Both engaged an argument that is larger than its participants: a working model of virtue.

My only object, I said, in continuing the discussion, has been the desire to ascertain the nature and relations of virtue; for if this were clear, I am very sure that the other controversy which has been carried on at length by both of us—you affirming and I denying that virtue can be taught—would also become clear. The result of our discussion appears to me to be singular. For if the argument had a human voice, that voice would be heard laughing at us and saying: 'Protagoras and Socrates, you are strange beings; there are you, Socrates, who were saying that virtue cannot be taught, contradicting yourself now by your attempt to prove that all things are knowledge, including justice, and temperance, and courage,—which tends to show that virtue can certainly be taught; for if virtue were other than knowledge, as Protagoras attempted to prove, then clearly virtue cannot be taught; but if virtue is entirely knowledge, as you are seeking to show, then I cannot but suppose that virtue is capable of being taught. Protagoras, on the other hand, who started by saying that it might be taught, is now eager to prove it to be anything rather than knowledge; and if this is true, it must be quite incapable of being taught. Now I, Protagoras, perceiving this terrible confusion of our ideas, have a great desire that they should be cleared up. And I should like to carry on the discussion until we ascertain what virtue is, and whether capable of being taught or not, lest haply Epimetheus should trip us up and deceive us in the argument, as he forgot us in the story; I prefer your Prometheus to your Epimetheus, for of him I make use, whenever I am busy about these questions, in Promethean care of my own life. And if you have no objection, as I said at first, I should like to have your help in the enquiry. (361a-361c)

If this dialogue is a private variation on the form of a public trial (as Scott Buchanan maintains), then the argument is prosecutor, and Socrates and Protagoras are equally tried.

2. A Science of Measurement

As previously noted, Plato set the dialogue just before the outbreak of the Peloponnesian War. Nussbaum points out that this establishes an impatience in readers who know what is coming, even though the participants do not, and establishes a greater degree of openness to what she calls "a pessimistic and radical doctor" for the city's ills (p. 91).

The Socrates of this dialogue is young, and Nussbaum focuses on the erotic gossip that serves as prelude, noting that this is a glimpse of Socrates before he was transformed by Diotima. The "science of measurement" in *Protagoras*, like that in *Symposium*, places personal physical beauty and the beauty of philosophy on a single quantitative scale. Nussbaum refers to *Charmides*, set at about the same time, in which Socrates "loses control" because of passion in the middle of a conversation in which he is insisting that the beauty of the body and the beauty of the soul are similar, the soul being more important (p. 92).

Nussbaum describes the encounter with Protagoras as a competition for the soul of Hippocrates (p. 93), similar to but not quite identical with Buchanan's private variation on the form of a public trial. Socrates makes reference to the young man's namesake, a contemporary who is still remembered as the "father" of medicine and whose name is associated with the famous oath at the heart of medical ethics, and proposes that philosophy is a science for healing the soul, just as medicine is a science for healing the body. This has interesting implications for philosophy—particularly ethics, given several thousand years of more or less unbroken discussion of medicine as art and as science, a discussion that has struggled to balance scientific precision and control with artful improvisation. The beginning of the dialogue pictures ordinary deliberation as "confused, unsystematic, and consequently lacking in control over both present and future" (p. 93). This is an interesting point, given the deployment of the Prometheus myth: Prometheus may be translated as "forethought," Epimetheus as "afterthought." They are sometimes used as contrasting symbols of careful deliberation and unplanned action. Plato's Socrates, preferring Prometheus to Epimetheus, sees this as symptomatic of the need for "an orderly procedure of choice that will save us from being buffeted by the 'appearances' of the moment" (p. 93).

Plato addresses three specific problems of *tuchē* (Nussbaum, pp. 93-94):

- vulnerability to luck through attachment to vulnerable objects and activities;
- pursuit of plural values; and
- the power of passion.

Those, Nussbaum says, are singled out as diseases (p. 94). The correct art or science of practical choice would be the one that could cure them. This sets up the competition between the art or science of Socrates and that of Protagoras. Protagoras and Socrates agree on the need for a *technē* but disagree on what that *technē* should be. In Nussbaum's reading, they agree in the end that it must be a practical science of the type favored by Socrates. Just what that type is must remain an open question for the moment.

In *Protagoras, technē* and *epistēmē* (knowledge) are used interchangeably (Nussbaum, p. 94). The ordinary conception of *technē* is shaped and displayed in the antithesis between *technē* and *tuchē*, the contrast between living at the mercy of *tuchē* and living a life made safer or more controlled by *technē*. *Technē* is a deliberate application of human intelligence to some part of the world, yielding some control over *tuchē*. The association of knowledge with control has had fateful consequences in the history of Western science (Merchant, 1990), though pinning that association on Socrates is problematic.

Nussbaum takes up the development of *technē* in Plato's student Aristotle, who, like any good student, did not simply follow his teacher. Drawing both on Aristotle and on medical texts extant in his time, she distinguishes four features of *technē*: universality, teachability, precision, and concern with explanation (p. 95). Universality involves judgments about whole classes of events rather than isolated events. Teachability requires that, while unordered experience can only be had, *technē* can be communicated in advance of experience. Precision requires that *technē* at least approach regularity even if it does not achieve it. A complete absence of regularity would be indicative of *tuchē*. Finally, *technē*, concerned with explanation, responds to "why" questions in contrast to the arbitrariness of *tuchē*. All four features bear on the goal of mastering contingency. With regard to practical reason, they seek "to eliminate some of the chanciness from human social life" (Nussbaum, p. 97). And, on the surface at least, they diminish the importance of improvisational aspects of Socratic discourse.

3. Living Life and Saving It

Turning from statements about *technē* to examples of *technai*, Nussbaum identifies three types (p. 98):

* Clearly productive ones where the product can be specified apart from knowledge of the craftsperson's activities (shoemaking, house building).
* Arts such as medicine where there is a vague end (health) towards which the practitioner's activity aims.
* Arts with purely internal ends (flute-playing, dancing, athletic achievement).

Protagoras favors staying close to the ordinary practice of deliberation, systematizing it only a little. Socrates favors a more radical scientific approach, a quantifiable art. The approach favored by Protagoras is conservative, and he understands human progress as a sort of tightwire between living life and saving it.

The myth in which Protagoras depicts the complex balancing act of human progress begins with creatures made from earth and fire, vulnerable to contingency. Prometheus and Epimetheus are charged with distributing to each species what it needs to survive. We are asked to imagine an uncharacterized object—a lump of earth and fire named "horse." This object is then given the arts and characteristics we associate with horses, such as speed, hooves, and oat-eating. We are invited to imagine that it could have been otherwise. The horse could have been given characteristics we associate with birds, for example. We discover that this is not so—if the "horse" had all the characteristics of a bird and none of the characteristics of a horse, it would simply be a bird (Nussbaum, p. 100). Arts were given to creatures to save the lives of those creatures, to make it possible for them to survive. But the arts in fact created creatures that had not previously existed. Continuing the story, we have creatures that look and act something like human beings for whom survival is tenuous at best. Though these creatures look and act something like human beings, they possess neither rationality nor social-political arts. The question is whether rationality and social-political arts are necessary characteristics of human being. Where these characteristics are lacking, is it possible to speak of human being at all (Nussbaum, pp. 101-102)?

Nussbaum notes two directions the story could take in its response to this question (p. 102):

* it could invite us to imagine coherently human life in which human beings lack justice and political institutions; or

- it could invite us to imagine that justice and political institutions so altered the creatures among whom they arose as to make them new, to make them human.

Protagoras leans toward this second approach: our nature is political. Hume's analysis would make justice external, in the service of human survival; but Protagoras makes it internal and aims toward civic virtue. For Protagoras, social excellence is to psychological nature as health is to bodily nature. His speech brings some key features of our practices of identifying individuals and kinds to the surface for critical reflection, in the process making us more aware of the social-political arts by which we already protect ourselves from contingency in the ordering of our cities (Nussbaum, p. 104). A clearer consciousness of those arts might give us standards for choosing among value alternatives. The relationship between improvisation and order is important here as well. Knowing arts by which we protect ourselves from contingency might diminish the effects of *tuchē*, but it would also diminish the possibility of improvisation necessary to conversation.

Turning to specific problems of *tuchē* enumerated earlier, there are clearly identifiable limits to progress toward control effected by Protagoras's approach (Nussbaum, pp. 104-105), which:

(1) "allows us to continue to value vulnerable activities and objects";
(2) keeps alive the possibility of tragedy by denying the unity of the virtues; and
(3) "recognizes the power of the passions as an ongoing danger for public morality."

Protagoras's *technē* follows Tiresias's advice: take small steps. Nussbaum attributes Protagoras's conservatism in part to his satisfaction with the life he has lived (p. 105), but the younger participants in the audience are not so satisfied. The more profound reason for Protagoras's conservatism, though, is his consciousness that a new art may mean a new being: what is intended to save human beings may make us something other than human beings (Nussbaum, p. 106). Here, two contemporary writers, Octavia Butler and Donna Haraway, take up the challenge imaginatively and philosophically. Haraway, in her "Cyborg Manifesto," pictures a humanity irretrievably transformed by the machines that we make extensions of our perceptual systems. Butler, in both utopian and dystopian visions of possible futures, ties humanity's survival into necessary processes of freely becoming other than we are. Neither proposes an uninterrupted march away from contingency as a desirable transformation.

4. Numbering and Knowing

A science of measurement is intended to make human beings capable of taking different things and "comparing them with respect to some property in which they are interested" (Nussbaum, p. 106). Socrates looked to this model in *Euthyphro*, a dialogue in which conversation about piety is predicated on the assumption that, in order to prosecute someone for impiety, one must know with precision what piety is—an assumption of more than passing importance, given the fact that Socrates himself stands accused of impiety. The connection between numbering and knowing has deep roots in Greek thought by the time of Plato (Nussbaum, p. 107). For Plato, there is no *technē* without number. Plato's argument develops a tradition that reaches back through Hippocrates and *Prometheus Bound* to Homer (at least to the eighth century BCE), drawing on a Pythagorean epistemology that equated the graspability of a thing with its countability. Deliberation as a kind of measuring is not alien to ordinary Greek thought, and it is probably even less alien to ours. Such a science would make incommensurable things commensurable, designate a single end, and make choice subject to clear public procedures (Nussbaum, pp. 108-109).

Nussbaum describes the end of Socrates's argument as a claim to have demonstrated the need for an ethical science of measurement (p. 109). She maintains that Socrates adopts pleasure as end in *Protagoras* strictly for the science it promises. The need for measurement motivates the search for an acceptable measure (pp. 109-110). This calls into question Mill's claim that Socrates is the originator of Utilitarianism, though it leaves intact the more modest claim that Socrates's argument is formally teleological. Nussbaum takes the absence of sustained discussion of the nature of pleasure as evidence that pleasure serves a place-holding function in the dialogue (p. 111). Socrates, in a pattern that Aristotle will later repeat, concedes at the end that the content of pleasure has been left unspecified; his point has been to establish the form of a science of measurement. Nussbaum notes parallels (to which I already alluded in the first chapter) with the nineteenth century drive toward utilitarianism and hedonism in Bentham and Henry Sidgwick (p. 112). Science is both continuous with ordinary belief and required to go beyond it; but note just how artful the science Socrates proposes is. It is not an end but a procedure for dialogue that includes the possibility of improvisation—asking and answering back, as Socrates put it. Control here consists in faithful adherence to a method, following the argument where it takes us, not in the mastery characteristic of a carefully constructed speech or a tightly written treatise.

5. Knowledge and Desire

Socrates and Protagoras explore the ethical dilemma posed by situations in which there is presumed to be a conflict between knowledge and desire. In such a situation, known as *akrasia*, a person can do either of two things. Socrates and Protagoras consider the instance in which the person, while knowing that the first thing is better, is overcome by pleasure and chooses the second. In their conversation, Socrates and Protagoras agree on two premises: pleasure is identical with the good, and the person caught in this presumed conflict between knowledge and desire believes pleasure to be identical with the good. Using these premises, Socrates exposes a logical absurdity by substituting "good" for "pleasant" in the statement of the problem: confronted with the possibility of doing one of two things, a person who knows that the first thing is more good than the second chooses the second because she or he is overcome by the good in it. The absurdity consists in choosing a smaller over a larger quantity of good. The mistake can only occur, Socrates says, because of mistaken judgment about the quantities. There is no conflict between knowledge and desire, only mistaken judgment resulting from deficient knowledge. Here, Socrates has assumed two further premises: when the person chooses, she or he weighs and measures by a single quantitative standard of value; and she or he chooses one thing over another only if she or he believes it to be more valuable. What Socrates really tells us, then, is that as long as rationality works it does not break down—not, by itself, a very helpful conclusion (Nussbaum, pp. 113-115).

But Socrates implies that acceptance of "the qualitative singleness and homogeneity of the values actually modifies the passions, removing the motivations we now have for certain sorts of irrational behavior" (Nussbaum, p. 115). To explain this, Nussbaum describes an ordinary case of *akrasia*: eat a bagel now, reducing the distance you can run and your overall health, or eat the bagel after you run. As she notes, the bagel does not look like a little packet of health or a little bit of exercise. It looks like a bagel, so you eat it. She then proposes a contrasting case: your rational principle is to maximize your bagel-eating. Standing in the middle of a room, you see on one side a plate containing two fresh buttered bagels, on the other side, an identical plate with one fresh buttered bagel. You can go for either plate but not both. You know you ought to go for the plate with two bagels, but—overcome by desire—you eat the one. Nobody who really saw the choices this way would choose in the way described. So what Socrates demonstrates is the connection between our *akrasia* problem and the way we see things. The perception of heterogeneity is a necessary condition for the development of irrational motivations. Get rid of heterogeneity and the irrational motivations will disappear (Nussbaum, pp. 115-116).

Socrates offers "a radical proposal for the transformation of our lives," though he represents it as an empirical description. This science "restructures our attachments so that they are far less fragile" (Nussbaum, p. 117). It eliminates particularity as a motivating factor. Socrates, Nussbaum maintains, "shows us what motivates a movement beyond the ordinary" (p. 117). He invites us to imagine a Socratic conclusion to the Protagorean story, and Nussbaum takes him up on the invitation. In this imagined conclusion, the Protagorean humans invent tragedy to show that their lives are not worth living. Then Apollo grants the science of deliberative measurement to humankind through his emissary Socrates. To the recipients of this gift, tragedies are simply incomprehensible (Nussbaum, pp. 117-119).

Nussbaum insists that the dialogue shows "more than a competition for a young soul." It shows "a tragedy of human practical reason," an appropriately ironic demonstration if the conclusion to the Protagorean story is that recipients of Apollo's gift find tragedy incomprehensible (p. 119). Plato tells us that "if part of our humanness is our susceptibility to certain sorts of pain, then the task of curing pain may involve putting an end to humanness" (p. 120). It is our very humanness, not some defect in our humanity, that drives us into pain and destruction. By definition, then, we are tragic heroes even when our lives and actions appear anything but heroic. We have a choice, but we have good reason to doubt our ability to choose.

Chapter Five

THE SHAPE OF CHARACTER

Aristotle's discussion of virtue in *Nicomachean Ethics* has been among the most influential in Western philosophy and theology. It shaped Thomas Aquinas's thought in ways that continue to exercise profound influence in Roman Catholic social teaching, and, in spite of Martin Luther's often caustic dismissal of Aristotle and the Scholastic tradition, it has left its mark on Protestant thinking as well. More recently, theologians and philosophers such as Stanley Hauerwas and Alasdair MacIntyre have returned to Aristotle for guidance in their constructions of virtue and narrative ethics.

As Plato and Aristotle tell their stories, reinventing and reinterpreting their heroic tradition, the virtues come to be defined as dispositions to act and to feel in particular ways. "To act virtuously," MacIntyre writes, is not "to act against inclination; it is to act from inclination formed by the cultivation of the virtues" (MacIntyre, p. 149). What is at stake in each of our actions is the kind of persons we will become. An adequate account of virtue requires an account of character that describes its genesis, including a description of how inclination is formed, and its relation to social structure.

1. Prudence

In the heroic society of Homeric epic, the relation is self-evident; but Plato and Aristotle, responding both to the Sophists and to the poets of Greek drama, make it a problem to be explored. In the conception of virtue that grew out of the conversation initiated by Homer and continued through the Sophists, Plato, Aristotle, and the tragic poets—especially Sophocles, judgment has a role for virtuous persons that it could not have for persons who are merely law-abiding (MacIntyre, p. 154).

Phronesis (practical wisdom), the Greek term which lies behind the Latin *prudentia* and the English "prudence," designates "someone who knows how to exercise judgment in particular cases" (MacIntyre, p. 154), including the kinds of cases described in Nussbaum's discussion of *Protagoras*. MacIntyre cautions that prudence can degenerate into "a certain cunning capacity for linking means to any end rather than to those ends which are genuine goods" (MacIntyre, p. 154), a problem highlighted by the place-holding function of pleasure in *Protagoras*. As Josef Pieper notes, this caution was already present in Thomas Aquinas's treatment of "false prudences." Thomas (1225-1274) speaks of "the 'prudence of the flesh,'" which, "instead of serving the true end of all human life...is directed solely toward the goods of the body" (Pieper, p. 19). False prudences, in Aquinas's view, arise from covetousness, which means "immoderate straining" for all the possessions which one thinks are needed to assure "importance and status" (Pieper, p. 21).

Aristotle connects intellectual virtues to virtues of character by way of perception, a connection with which we are already familiar because of Nussbaum's discussion of *akrasia* and the way we see things. The virtuous person does not need to reason to the mean but immediately perceives it. Prudence, as practical intelligence, is a structure of action that makes it possible to put all the other virtues into practice: it is a structure or state that makes it possible not only to see but also to embody the whole in the parts. It is particular in the same way that particular goods are particular; and, as noted earlier, it involves seeing into the heart of things.

MacIntyre reads actions as conclusions to practical syllogisms (MacIntyre, p. 161), which have four parts:

(1) the agent's "wants and goals";
(2) a major premise: doing a particular kind of action is the type of thing that is likely to achieve presupposed wants and goods;
(3) a minor premise: this particular action is an instance of the requisite kind; and
(4) a conclusion—the action itself.

For MacIntyre, ethics seeks to form character in ways that predispose agents toward actions which conclude practical syllogisms grounded in a true vision of human good. He defines ethics as "the education of the passions into conformity with pursuit of what theoretical reasoning identifies as the *telos* and practical reasoning as the right action to do in each particular time and place" (MacIntyre, p. 162), then identifies three "areas of questioning" that look more like imperatives for ethical research. We need, he says:

(1) "a teleological account" to replace Aristotle's "metaphysical biology";
(2) an adequate account of the relationship of ethics to the structure of the *polis*, a search for social-political forms "in and through which the kind of self which can exemplify the virtues can be found and educated and in which that self can find its arena"; and
(3) a more adequate understanding of the role of conflict (MacIntyre, pp. 162-163).

MacIntyre asks whether we can reconcile Aristotle with Sophocles. Nussbaum reads Aristotle as a reconciliation of the tragedy of human reason depicted in

Plato with the tragic vision of dramatists such as Sophocles; but MacIntyre sees Aristotle himself as needing reconciliation, particularly with regard to the relationship between conflict and vision of the good. Conflict, MacIntyre maintains, makes an important contribution to the formation of vision. Creating institutions within which the practice of virtue can flourish requires creation of "the right kinds of tension," the kinds of tension present in dynamic structures that neither simply disintegrate nor simply determine the substructures that they contain. Aristotle's *telos* is not a future end but a present one realized "in the way our whole life is constructed" (MacIntyre, p. 175).

MacIntyre traces three conceptions of virtue that have dominated Western tradition. First is the heroic conception articulated in the Homeric epics, in which virtue is a quality that enables an individual "to discharge his or her social role." Second is the Aristotelian vision adopted into Christianity by way of Aquinas, in which virtue is a quality that enables an individual "to move towards the achievement of the specifically human *telos*, whether natural or supernatural." Third is the peculiarly American pragmatism identified with Ben Franklin, in which virtue is a quality that has utility in achieving earthly and heavenly success. These do not simply supplant one another in succession, but are subsumed in a developmental logic consisting of three stages applied in every complete account of virtue: first, a background account of "practice"; second, a description of the narrative order of a single human life; and, third, an account of moral tradition. A practice is defined as "any coherent and complex form of socially established cooperative human activity through which goods internal to that form of activity are realized in the course of trying to achieve those standards of excellence which are appropriate to, and partially definitive of, that form of activity, with the result that human powers to achieve excellence, and human conceptions of the ends and goods involved, are systematically extended" (MacIntyre, p. 187).

Based on this definition of practice and his account of the moral tradition of the West, MacIntyre offers a first definition of virtue as "an acquired human quality the possession and exercise of which tends to enable us to achieve those goods which are internal to practices and the lack of which effectively prevents us from achieving any such goods" (MacIntyre, p. 191). He cautions against confusing practices either with sets of technical skills or with institutions. Virtues maintain an ordered relationship among skills, practices, and institutions.

2. The Order of That Which Has Parts

Common usage connects virtue with human dependability and locates it both in use and in social action. Plato's distinction between being good at a particular skill and being good as a human being poses the moral problem of good human use not only of things but also of one's power—in relation to things, to self, and to others. For Aristotle, virtue is a special kind of quality designated most often by *hexis* but also by *ethos*, custom. Virtue is closely related to habit, which is not an activity, but a disposition to act (Simon, p. 51). Yves Simon calls it an "intermediary potency," like recitation of poetry, midway between a natural ability to learn lines and their actual recitation (p. 52).

Simon reminds us that, while we might think we can discover "actual relations of things," all we can ever know for sure are "the habits of our mind" (p. 52). He follows Hume in asserting that the necessity of habit is not objective, then takes the additional step of insisting that, although moral action resembles habit, "truly moral action is never involuntary" (p. 55). He distinguishes *hexis*, which W.D. Ross translates as "state of character," from habit. Simon shies away from Ross's translation because of its static implications. He proposes a distinction between habit, in which necessity is subjective, and *habitus*, in which necessity is objective. "Habit," he says, "relieves us of the need to think; but *habitus* makes us think creatively" (p. 60).

Aristotle and Plato agree that knowledge (*epistēmē*) is possible only of what is objectively necessary, while we can only have opinion (*doxa*) of things that can be otherwise. Recall that *technē* and *epistēmē* are used interchangeably in *Protagoras*, connecting knowledge with predictability and control. Simon insists that "even the best judgments in matters of opinion should be uttered according to the remarkable formula sometimes used by Scholastic writers: *cum foridime alterius*, that is, 'with the fear (or better, with the reservation) that it could turn out otherwise'" (Simon, p. 63). Socratic wisdom has often been understood as demanding the same of what we presume to know. This is also the import of tragic vision—not fear so much as expectation: it could be otherwise.

The stability of habit makes it "second nature." As social animals, human beings acquire many characteristics non-naturally; but these are not characteristics that it is not in the nature of human beings to have (Hutchinson, 1986). This is important in distinguishing the classical view from that of Kant: Kant separates morality from nature while the classical view connects them. As *habitus*, virtue is *diathesis* (disposition), defined by Aristotle as "the order of that which has parts" (*Metaphysics*, Book V).

3. Vulnerability

Aristotle returns to and further articulates many of the insights of tragedy with regard to the proper relation of human being to *tuchē*. His philosophy is also in part a critique of what Nussbaum refers to as Plato's conception of philosophy as radical life-saver. Aristotle criticizes Plato's understanding of the task of philosophy as being to subdue *tuchē*, concluding instead that the best human life is vulnerable to catastrophe. His method, reminiscent of tragic drama in intent if not in style, is to set down appearances, then work through the difficulties they present (Nussbaum, pp. 240-263). Applying this method now would mean assembling a range of common beliefs, then finding an account that comprehends all of them. As Nussbaum describes it (pp. 245-248), Aristotle's philosophical method circumscribes itself by the ordinary in a "rich account of philosophical procedure and philosophical limits" consisting of five steps:

- set down the relevant appearances;
- set out the puzzles or dilemmas with which they confront us;
- seek consistency: solve the puzzles;
- bring the solutions back to the appearances. "Theory must remain committed to the ways human beings live, act, see—to the *pragmata*, broadly construed" (Nussbaum, p. 247); and
- decide which appearances to keep and which to discard: nothing universally believed is entirely discarded; nothing that we have to be using to argue or inquire can get thrown out.

By choosing appearances as his philosophical paradigm, Nussbaum argues, Aristotle confronts earlier Greek tradition, for which appearance is opposed to truth, and sides with Protagoras against both Plato and Plato's Socrates. Plato sought eternal, stable starting points; but Aristotle insists that he will find his truth inside what we say, see, and believe, rather than outside. He reminds us of the humanness of good science, describing the world as it appears to members of "our kind" (Nussbaum, p. 245). By sometimes interchanging *endoxa* (common beliefs on a subject) and *phainomena* (appearances), Aristotle lays the groundwork for a conversational approach that, though not presented as explicitly as Plato's, is equally dialogical. Aristotle starts with what his opponent says, then seeks to bring "the isolated person into line" (Nussbaum, pp. 252-253). Nussbaum reads this as an invitation to the other "to accept our fellowship." If the other "is a skeptic bent on securing his equanimity against the risks attendant on community and human involvement, he will refuse that. We cannot, in any harder sense, show him that he is *wrong*" (Nussbaum, p. 253). Speaking or acting enmeshes one in the world of appearances: to avoid appearances, one must reduce oneself to silence and immobility. For this reason,. Aristotle does not accuse his opponent of being wrong, but of being comical.

Discourse is bounded by the experience of the group: "We can have truth only *inside* the circle of the appearances, because only there can we communicate, even refer, at all" (Nussbaum, p. 257). This leads to realism, not idealism, skepticism, or empiricism. More importantly, it connects Aristotle's argument (like Kierkegaard's) with communication. Any new view must be commended to our attention by showing its relationship to our experience. Nussbaum depicts Aristotle as affirming the importance of the ordinary. Is philosophy the domain of "a certain tribe of strange professionals"? Aristotle clearly says no: philosophy is a common pursuit that has its origin in wonder. "We need philosophy to show us the way back to the ordinary and to make it an object of interest and pleasure, rather than contempt and evasion," Nussbaum says (p. 260). "The most serious obstacle to good philosophy," she writes, "is not ignorance, but bad philosophy, which captivates by its pleasing clarity" (p. 262).

In Aristotle, there is a spectrum, "from animal action through animal-like human action, to rational and virtuous human action" (Nussbaum, p. 267). These types of actions have four common points:

- motion is explained by ascribing a complex of desires and beliefs or perceptions;
- factors are intentional;
- there is a logical and causal connection with a goal; and
- physiology is mentioned not in response to "why" but to "how."

A two-fold philosophical background lies behind this discussion: materialism and idealism stand against ordinary accounts. The natural science tradition before Aristotle gives physiological accounts, resulting in reductionist scientism. Aristotle objects to neglect of explanation other than material, which he says results in a loss of distinctions and detachment from the richness of ordinary talk. One variation on the loss of distinction is that between movements for which there is a why and those for which there is not. This criticism begins in Plato and is amplified by Aristotle (Nussbaum, pp. 269-289).

4. Active Desire

Plato and his predecessors assume a choice between explanation by physiology and explanation by reason. Intellectualist readings such as that of Plato are marked by:

(1) sharp distinction between humans and other animals;
(2) sharp distinction between actions motivated by choice and other actions; and
(3) loss of customary distinction between chosen movements and other movements.

Plato posits activity of intellect, passivity of desire. Nussbaum takes up the discussion of desire by noting that the philosopher must sometimes step in and create a term of art to "enable us to recognize the salient features of our antecedent conception and to defend it against superficially attractive philosophical rivals." She credits Aristotle with coining *orexis*—a new term for the active desire characteristic of moral activity—from *oregō*, an old term meaning to extend one's hand. Euripides and Thucydides had already transferred *oregō* to an inner, psychological realm. The verb strongly implies directedness toward an object, and it is active: "object-directed, active inner reaching out" (Nussbaum, p. 275). Aristotle criticizes Plato's familiar tripartite division of the soul: every part of the soul is orectic. What animals have in common is that we reach out. In this regard, it is interesting that the beginning of human development in Piaget's theory is the primary circular reaction, a built-in reaching out mechanism with which the equilibration of cognitive structures begins in the construction of physical knowledge.

Aristotle's biological account, problematic as it may be in matters of content, has the distinct advantage of drawing human beings close to other animals. There are, he writes, two sources of animal movement: cognition (*noēsis*) and desire (*orexis*). In order for movement to occur, the good, associated with desire, and the possible, associated with cognition, must come together (Nussbaum, p. 275). To say that we do not fly because we do not have wings may have been convincing as a causal account to Aristotle's original audience. But he does not accept such physiological description as causal, and we (who do fly) certainly should not. Physiological factors are not causes; they are more proper to how than to why. That we are not born with wings puts limits on our modes of locomotion that birds, for example, do not experience. That this is more relevant to how than to why is evidenced by the history of human flight. If we were built differently, we might also fly differently. Desire, Aristotle maintains, is what imparts movement. *Hekousios*, voluntary movement, is distinguished from *akousios*, automatic movement. *Hekousios* is appropriate for ethical assessment, *akousios* is not.

Nussbaum proposes Aristotle's common account as an alternative to a Kantian-Platonist dichotomy in which only two choices exist: brutish or rational. Aristotle's common account includes a "natural animal basis for the development of moral character" (p. 285). There is a kind of "reasonableness to the appetitive forces themselves" (p. 286). The strongest claim to truth rests in clear articulation of appearances. Practical deliberation, Aristotle insists, is not scientific; but it is the appropriate mode of deliberation for ethics. By maintaining an interplay of universal rule and particular perception, he constructs a view of good within appearances. Ethics is anthropocentric, and its goal is practical, not theoretical. Socrates argued in *Protagoras* for an anthropocentric ethic that is also scientific, but Aristotle insists that ethics is inherently unscientific because of the inescapable problem of measurement and commensurability in ethics. The qualitative variety and observer-relativity of pleasure are good reasons not to base an ethical science on it; but Aristotle's opposition to ethics as *techne* goes beyond the argument against hedonism. The specificity of the virtues calls the very possibility of a science of ethics into question. But Aristotle's emphasis on means reintroduces the possibility of measurement. He does not say that we deliberate about means but that we deliberate about what pertains to the end. In saving appearances, Aristotle restores polytheism against Plato's monotheistic thrust (Nussbaum, pp. 294-297). I will return to this tension between polytheism and monotheism later.

The Platonic scientist looks for regularity as a way to ensure that she or he will never be taken by surprise. Vulnerability is seen as an unfortunate consequence of ethical particularity. Rules may be guidelines, or they may themselves be the ultimate authorities. The second possibility promises a science, the first does not. Rules of the first sort are not incompatible with Aristotle's non-scientific understanding of ethics. Aristotle stresses that an anthropocentric ethics will rely more firmly on its standing rules than a Platonic conception, because there is no universal to fall back on. Practical wisdom uses rules as summaries or guides; it is like perceiving, a two way illumination between particular and universal (Nussbaum, pp. 298-306).

Passion is an important part of good deliberation because of its motivational role, a point also made by Hans Furth in his study of Piaget and Freud. Choice lies on the borderline between the intellectual and the passional. The well formed character is a unity of thought and desire, and perception is a complex response of the entire personality.

To give priority to the general sacrifices the ethical value of surprise, contextuality, and particularity. Aristotle returns to a prephilosophic acknowledgment of contingent particulars that renounces the Platonic aspiration to control. There is a certain circularity in this process, but, as Nussbaum notes, there is nothing inherently wrong with circularity: the question is whether the circle is "small and pernicious" or "large and interesting" (p. 312)

5. Perception and Passion

In Euripides's (480-406 BCE) drama, Hecuba's response to her grandson Astyanax's murder is no theory. She does not presume to rise above the human. She has no measuring scale, no reductive device, only what Nussbaum calls the "yielding responsiveness" of a humanly valuable response, "a flexible movement back and forth between particular and general," with particular having priority. Hecuba "binds herself to the possibility of loss" (Nussbaum, pp. 313-317; pp. 397-421). I will return to *Hecuba* later, in Chapter Nine.

Because external goods—subject to luck—are necessary for happiness, the good human life is necessarily vulnerable. Aristotle lays out two extremes: either the good life is simply equal to good fortune (luck), or luck has no power to influence the goodness of human life (Nussbaum, p. 319). Neither is entirely wrong. Life is made worth living by voluntary actions, though luck is a serious influence in the good life. Aristotle sympathizes with those who seek to make the good life invulnerable, but he contends that reduced vulnerability is the best we can hope for. Aristotle maintains that *eudaimonia* requires activity; a good state is not enough. *Eudaimonia* cannot be simply a *hexis*: action is essential for praiseworthiness (Nussbaum, p. 324). The good condition is incomplete without action. *Eudaimonia* is complete. Goodness impeded and cut off is not praiseworthy. Being active means being open and, hence, vulnerable. Both *eudaimonia* and *makariotes* can be damaged by luck (Nussbaum, p. 330). A stable good life based on steady character is nonetheless vulnerable. Catastrophes can pollute good activity, so Aristotelian practical excellence "is prepared for the contingencies of the world and is not easily diminished by them" (Nussbaum, p. 333). A person of good and stable character will not act diametrically against character, so character is tolerably but not completely stable (Nussbaum, pp. 318-342).

6. The Necessity of Experience

Greek thinking was obsessed with the fragility of human existence, but the tragedy of the twentieth century has been deepened by the equally ominous specter of total control. Fragility is a relentless reminder that it may turn out otherwise. Total control is the equally relentless threat that it may not.

There is an old joke that begins with a person trapped in a fortune-cookie factory with no hope of escape apart from sending out messages inside the cookies (Reed, p. 68). Like most jokes and most tragedies, this one depends on an account of human experience that has the ring of truth. It rings true on at least two counts, both relevant to the discussion of freedom and necessity: the sense of being trapped and, more specifically, trapped in a factory, and the suspicion that the only potential contact with an outside is so thoroughly inscrutable as to be meaningless. What would you do if you opened a fortune cookie and read a message that said, "Help! I'm a prisoner in the factory where this cookie was made"? Reed finds it disconcerting that the image conveyed by the joke is so often used without humor to describe our daily lives (p. 68). This is reflective of what he calls the increasing barbarism of daily life, which he traces to rampant "degradation of opportunities for primary experience" (p. 5), a genealogy that presupposes J.J. Gibson's distinction between primary and secondary experience.

That Reed slides easily between experience and information is a sign of the times in which he writes: it is a truism that we live in an age of information, where every experience is an act of communication. But progress in information technology has not necessarily been matched by progress in communication. Reed complains that we spend billions on a superhighway that carries every kind of information except the ecological information "that allows us to experience things for ourselves" (p. 2). In a pattern familiar to those of us who have lived our lives in cities shaped by automobiles, the line of the highway traces a virtually impermeable wall. While (sometimes) increasing access to processed information, which Reed equates with "selected, modified, packaged, and presented" information, it (almost always) decreases access to ecological information. Ecological information is primary "for understanding our place in the world," while "processed information" is secondary: "It is this relation between primary and processed experience, in which the balance should be tilted toward primary experience, that has been disrupted and degraded by modern life" (p. 2). The superhighway that packages and delivers information in ever increasing quantities is a wall that deprives us of access to unpackaged, unprocessed information. It places us with inescapably Kafkaesque efficiency at the same time that it deprives us of the information we need to understand our place in the world. Our places become prisons, our images predictably claustrophobic. This cuts us entirely loose from the concept of virtue in heroic societies: mechanisms that efficiently place us simultaneously deny access to knowledge that would enable us to critically assess the significance of place.

Parallel to the distinction between primary and secondary experience is a distinction between ordinary and exotic experience. Reed assumes that while primary experience is more ordinary and secondary experience more exotic, modern life has inverted the relationship and devalued the ordinary, a complaint that echoes Aristotle's objection to the dismissal of appearances by his philosophical predecessors.

Reed argues that processed information can only lead to secondhand, indirect knowledge. He illustrates the distinction by contrasting the experience of looking at a face with the experience of looking at a photograph:

> No matter how thoroughly I scrutinize the photograph, at some point I stop learning about you and begin to learn about the picture (its graininess, color, light values). But when I meet you face to face there is no limit to the possibilities of exploration and discovery. (p. 3)

One of the criticisms that ecological theories of perception such as Reed's (and closely related pragmatic and phenomenological theories) have routinely encountered is that of naive realism. Reed readily embraces the realist label. But the problem is whether any experience is direct—and encountering a face can very quickly bring this to a head: if we do not go beyond the face, we are no better informed about the person than if we do not go beyond the picture.

Unlimited possibilities of exploration and discovery are no more likely to leap out of a face to face encounter than out of an encounter with a picture. In both cases, it is wise to consider possibilities bounded even if we wish to entertain the possibility that they are infinite. Reed touches on this problem in his description of the prospective character of human experience, reminiscent of Aristotle's description of animals, including human beings, as orectic: the challenge is to construct an account of the world in which every present encounter is as pregnant with future as it is heavy with past.

John Searle proposed a thought experiment that is a variation on the fortune cookie joke: Imagine an English-speaking person in a room with no exit. The room is empty except for a device that periodically dispenses papers with marks on them, a book or manual of some sort, and writing materials. Because there is nothing else to do and nowhere else to go, the person studies the papers coming into the room but does not understand the writing they contain, which looks like Chinese ideograms. Upon examining the book, she discovers that it also contains the marks that are on the papers coming into the room. The marks are in columns arranged in parallel with columns of English words. Because there is nothing else to do and nowhere else to go, she takes the papers coming into the room, finds the marks in the manual, and writes the corresponding English words next to the marks on the paper. She discovers what looks like a mail slot in the wall of the room and, after looking up the marks and writing the corresponding English words on the papers, places them in the slot. She continues to do this with all of the papers that come into the room (Reed, pp. 72, 73; Searle, 1984).

From the outside—to a person who did not know or did not care that another person was trapped inside—the room would look like a device for turning Chinese ideograms into English equivalents. Its efficiency would not require that the person inside the room understand Chinese (and it would be a singularly ineffective mechanism for teaching Chinese). Its efficiency would be profoundly diminished if the room had an exit—or if the person trapped inside decided to write her own messages on the papers she dispensed to the outside (or if someone on the outside read, understood, or responded to her messages).

"Looked at from the worker's point of view," Reed writes, "the fundamental goal of modern management is to make all jobs resemble the ones in Searle's prison" (p. 73). And the goal of modern schooling is to ensure that students destined to end up inside the box will not write their own messages nor will those destined to end up outside the box read or respond to them. Reed comments early in the book that

although we like to think of the post-World War II era as an age of democracy and opportunity, few of the major innovations in social institutions or organizations in these years have resulted in more *shared* experience or responsibility. Improvements in the access of individuals to social and economic resources have occurred in the context of increasingly large-scale and stratified social organizations. Nondemocratic institutions—megacorporations, large schools, entertainment conglomerates, and prisons—have begun to fill the available social space, dominating the daily life of individuals and crowding out opportunities for autonomous or grassroots activities and experience. (p. 6)

Reed's point is not to call for a return to some supposed golden age of democracy and community but to identify the post-World War II era as a containment culture intended to put people in our place and keep us there—a function it has performed with devastating efficiency. As Alan Nadel puts it, "from the first atomic bomb tests to Vietnam, 'democracy' has named stories produced under the rubric of containment" (Nadel, pp. 7-8). Stories produced under the rubric of containment have meticulously signified nothing as a strategy of containment, an epistemology of the closet that, by repetition of tropes, struggles endlessly to keep the narrative straight. "History is a cipher for omission" (Nadel, p. 8); reading, writing, and living it (not three activities, but one) involves seeing (as Wallace Stevens eloquently put it) nothing that is not there and the nothing that is.

Nadel evokes Salman Rushdie, who has been concerned in much of his work with seeing what is right before our eyes, especially in the context of total states from Ayatollah Khomeini's Iran to Margaret Thatcher's Britain, referring to *Midnight's Children* in the course of recounting a personal anecdote that frames his book as an act of remembering. For Nadel, as for Rushdie, the connection between "national trauma" and "personal narratives" is beyond the scope of the book but "informs virtually every page" (p. xi). Nadel, like Rushdie, is concerned with absences that are uncannily present. That Saleem, the main character of *Midnight's Children*, is "handcuffed to history" is signified by the coincidence of his birth with the birth of India: both occurred on 15 August 1947—as did Nadel's birth. This is an important indicator of how Nadel occupies a past that occupies his present and ours.

For Nadel, as for the postmodern writers he calls to mind, history is an accomplice: "Postmodern writers…realize that they have complete control over history and no control whatsoever over events" (p. 39). To write that writing is simultaneously "a source of truth" and "a process of distortion" (p. 66), is to place oneself in a position like the one he attributes to "the Western man": "The success of the Western man is measured by his ability to create a place in which there is no longer any place for him" (p. 193). Nadel ends by writing that his book "has been about narratives that effected strategies of containment in America during the decades immediately following World War II." Had those strategies "worked effectively," he writes, "this book would be illegible" (p. 297).

If the book is illegible, then the strategies "worked." If it is legible—or, as Nadel more confidently claims, because it *is* legible—the strategies did not work.

But if the effectiveness of the strategies is to be measured by their creation of places in which there is no longer any place, they have succeeded spectacularly: their end is the end of the world as we know it, "not a renunciation of cold war thematics" but

> a shift from the dominance of thematic narratives to the dominance of formal ones. The cold war will not have been put behind us by postmodern discourse, but it may be always and readily available as an in-the-wings or on-line performance whose cogency, like that of all other cultural narratives, will depend on its ability to conform to the codes of representation rather than to some historical referent. In such circumstances, nostalgia is passé, because the past is now. (Nadel, pp. 299-300)

—and the "end" is still the end of the world as we know it.

Reed's map of philosophy makes realism, not containment, the pivotal issue: on one side is realism (identified with experience and—later—William James's radical empiricism), while on the other is Cartesian rationalism. Cartesian rationalism was built on a systematic suspicion of the senses that led to an ever widening separation between the philosopher-scientist and the world—and a corresponding separation between philosophy or science and the ordinary experience of ordinary persons in the world.

Crucial to Reed's account is a seventeenth century change in the meaning of *idea*. As the influence of the new philosophy of Cartesianism grew, what Thomas Reid criticized as the "ideal theory" relocated ideas from essences beyond (beneath, behind, above) the world to intermediaries (between person and world) inside the head. Earlier, we saw this clearly in Locke. Since Descartes (1596-1650), Western philosophy has tended to assume that what we experience is internal (in the mind), not external (in the world). Descartes separated perception into experience and judgment, privileging judgment and withdrawing from experience. In fact, as numerous commentators have noted, one was considered philosophical or rational in much of the Western tradition only to the extent that one withdrew (abstracted) from ordinary experience (Lloyd, 1993).

Reed's historical account moves quickly from Descartes to Kant, who proposed empirical realism combined with transcendental idealism, though his followers have tended to read him as an empirical idealist. Reed identifies two metaphysical strands coming out of Kant, one associated with Arthur Schopenhauer (1788-1860) that dismisses primary experience as appearance, and one associated with Hegel that identifies primary experiences (appearances) as contradictions to be overcome. Different though the two strands may be, Reed maintains that their shared legacy is a disdain for primary experience—which again recalls Aristotle's attempt to save appearances.

Consistent with Reed's emphasis on the social character of human being, though the mind is not in the head it most certainly is in the world. In the epilogue, "Fighting for Experience," Reed writes that "this book is about how we are losing our minds" (Reed, p. 158). To the extent that the Cartesian legacy is withdrawal from the world, such a loss is as predictable as it is devastating.

When Reed turns from diagnosis to prescription, he sets out to connect experience with the birth of hope. To do this, he turns first to John Dewey's insistence that freedom is more than unrestrained pursuit of self-interest: it is an exercise of power that is social to the core (Reed, p. 128). But he also returns to the bleak inversion characteristic of modern life in which claustrophobic images routinely elicit glimmers of recognition. In this regard, Dilbert's appearance on the cover of *Newsweek* is every bit as important as Beckett or Kafka. And he turns again to art and artists, specifically Bertolt Brecht and Pablo Picasso, motivated by his recognition of the need to work within existing patterns of experience that are permeated by what William Leach has described as a "brokering style" marked by routine repression of conviction and judgment in the interest of forging profitable relationships (Reed, p. 136). Most of the artists to whom Reed refers favorably throughout the book—beginning with the dedication to Victor Jara, Bob Marley, and Pete Seeger, and continuing through the discussion of Brecht—are widely recognized as political. But Beckett, Kafka, Picasso, and Jimi Hendrix are less likely to be recognized as such. Reed's reference to Picasso is direct, a quotation from a statement issued in the mid-1940s: "painting is not there merely to decorate the walls of flats. It is a means of waging offensive and defensive war against the enemy" (p. 160).

Hendrix is the source of Reed's title for the first chapter of the book, "Have You Ever Been Experienced?" Reed cites the song from which that question is quoted as evidence of the shift away from ordinary experience to exotic, from primary to secondary. But Hendrix's answer—dripping with irony—is as primary as it could possibly be: "Are you experienced? Have you ever *been* experienced? Well I have; let me prove it to you," followed by a brief but convincing demonstration of guitar virtuosity. Even a casual listener knows Jimi Hendrix is experienced, has been experienced, because she or he has experienced him. His instantly recognizable performance of the "Star-Spangled Banner" is an even more obvious example of waging offensive and defensive war against the enemy. This is what Beckett, Kafka, and Hendrix have in common that is crucial if Reed's argument is to be more than a counsel of despair: all of them were masters at telling stories from inside prisons where there is nothing to tell.

Chapter Six

THE SHAPE OF THE CITY

In the *Republic*, Plato launches a Western tradition of constructing ideal cities as critical tools for thinking about actual ones, particularly actual ones that resemble the prisons of the previous chapter. That the *Republic* was written in the aftermath of the Peloponnesian War, probably after the first of Plato's expeditions to Syracuse as an advisor to the tyrant of that city-state, is indicative of his concern with practical problems of philosophy. The formula proposed in the *Republic*, that a just state is possible only where philosophers become rulers, is the outcome of reflection on a practical problem posed both by the effects of a protracted war and by the challenge of politics in the Greek world of Plato's time.

The dialogue is set in a time of truce during the Peloponnesian War, a war that shattered Plato's world. Writing in its aftermath, he recalls the relative peace that emerged from time to time during the protracted struggle. Socrates reflects with others on the meaning and possibility of justice in a temporary and relative peace that Plato knows is to be shattered in exactly the same way that Socrates's life was brought to an end—by the same Athens that epitomized the best of Greece, the "Hellas of Hellas" as Thucydides had Pericles say.

Plato saw a fundamental contradiction in his own context, very much like the contradiction that drives Greek tragedy: the best of his world was responsible for the destruction of his world. That contradiction confronted him with a problem, but it also helped him shape Socrates's seemingly contradictory self-understanding as a philosopher who knew nothing. In Socrates, this led to the realization that the argument, in the image adopted, as we have seen, at the end of *Protagoras*, is perfectly capable of laughing at those who participate in it. For Plato, this pointed to something beyond the disputants who shattered their own world.

Plato's shattered world, with the process by which it was shattered, is a framework within which to understand the world-shattering paradox of Socrates's style as well as the world-shattering paradox of his death. At the same time, Socrates's paradoxical self-understanding is a framework within which to describe the process by which worlds are shattered.

1. A Hunt

The *Republic* begins with an offering to Artemis—a strange starting point for politics, but not for a hunt. It is both appropriate and pious to begin an activity with a sacrifice to the deity associated with the activity. This activity is at least partly independent of its participants, and the process is at least as important as its product. Hence it is the deity associated with the process, not the product, to whom sacrifice is made.

When discussion of justice begins, it is placed in the hands not of Cephalus, but of his heir, Polemarchus, a fact noted with amusement by both Socrates and Cephalus. It begins after a discussion of the detachment that grows out of inherited wealth. Polemarchus pursues the argument (his inherited wealth) in much the same way one pursues the fox in a fox hunt—for recreation as much as for capture. As in *Protagoras*, Socrates emphasizes process and procedure over product. The point is not to determine and defend an answer but to participate in a search for truth. Plato's Socrates professes reluctance to allow poets to ridicule gods and heroes, yet he is more than willing to have the argument ridicule anyone.

In the poetics outlined in Book III, Socrates maintains that all mythology and poetry is a narration of events, either past, present, or future. All narration is either simple narration, imitation, or a combination of the two. In simple narration, the narrator speaks as himself or herself; in imitation, the narrator speaks as someone else. Epic is simple narration, while tragedy and comedy are imitation. This means that Plato's work, which is not simple narration, must be either tragedy or comedy.

Plato's use of a mimetic form to argue against *mimesis* is ironic, whether it is a strategic move in which *mimesis* is deployed in a less than ideal state as a means to an end, the end being a state in which simple narration would suffice, or a simple demonstration of the power of *mimesis* which shows that even arguments against it must employ it. Either way, we have something very close to what Stanley Fish calls a "self-consuming artifact." A mimetic narrative that calls *mimesis* into question is the narrative equivalent of a philosopher who professes ignorance. The end of Book III reminds us that the city Socrates and his friends have been struggling to construct in imagination is built on a myth. The city designed to contain the mimetic threat is founded on *mimesis*. Constructing the just city calls the city and its justice into question. That question, part of the definition of justice, is an embodiment of Socratic irony.

The familiar story of the cave that Socrates constructs in Book VII is an even older joke than the one evoked in discussion of Reed. He imagines prisoners in an underground cave with an opening toward the light, chained in place, unable to move, so that all they can see are shadows of images carried by people behind them (the people themselves being blocked off by a low wall) cast on the wall in front of them by a fire blazing far away behind them. If they could talk with one another about what they saw, they would believe that they were talking about reality. Socrates enhances the image by speaking of an echo that would lead the prisoners to believe that voices and sounds came from the shadows. "To them," he points out, "the truth would be literally nothing but the shadows of the images."

Socrates invites us to imagine that the prisoners are released. Turned toward the light, they are blinded and confused. When images passing by are pointed out to them, they appear less real than the shadows to which they have grown accustomed. Forced to look at the light, the prisoners experience intense pain and struggle to turn back toward shadows, their truth. Compelled to come into the light of the sun itself, the prisoners experience still greater pain and irritation. They would become accustomed to this world only gradually. After a time, they would be able to see objects in the light of day. Then, gradually, they would be able to see the sun in its own proper place. At length, they would begin to reason about the sun as the source of all that they had been accustomed to seeing.

If a person who had gone through this experience of liberation were put back in the cave, she or he would be very slow to perceive the old realities. It would be difficult to see at all under those conditions. Others who had remained in the cave would think him or her ridiculous at best, dangerous at worst. They would be convinced that she or he had gone up, then come down "without eyes." They would be convinced that it would be best not to even think about going up. This poses the problem of defining the art by which a soul may be turned toward the light. Given our existence in the cave, how are we to use shadows to communicate the existence of light, of images, and of reality? How do we tell a story in a prison where there is nothing to tell?

Every object, Socrates tells us, has an essence created by God. Objects, in turn, are made, and they participate in the essence that is common to all similar objects. Those who make these objects are really creators. One could say that they are similar to God in this process of creation. Even though producers create nothing but images, they do create; so they are only once removed from the realm of truth. Works of art, on the other hand, imitate objects. The artist or poet, then, is not a maker but an imitator. Twice removed from the realm of truth, she or he imitates appearance only, not reality. This marks the rejection of appearance to which Aristotle later objects.

But the criterion by which Socrates judges producers and imitators in this account is a type of utility or practicality; it is not the criterion he used in judging the various mathematical disciplines, nor is it the criterion used in judging philosophy. Poetry and other mimetic arts are despised because they do not participate in transformation of the world or construction of the world in conformity with the world of essences. Various mathematical arts are valued because they do not concern themselves with the world, but deal with essences only. In one case, noninvolvement with the phenomenal world is criticized. In the other it is praised. Why?

I suggest that Plato has made a creative mimetic comment on *mimesis*. Deploying it consciously, he condemns its unconscious deployment. The poet as surely as the ruler must be a philosopher. This is illustrated by the myth of Er, with which the dialogue ends. Whatever one's lot, the practice of virtue makes it good—and the practice of virtue derives from the practice of philosophy. Bear in mind that the term philosophy was coined to distinguish the philosopher—who claims a passion for wisdom—from the sophist—who claims to be wise. A philosopher can (like Plato) use mimetic arts to relativize *mimesis*, to turn the soul toward the world of essences, and to engage the world in a practice of philosophy that changes the world. Plato's myth does not allow those who have entered the realm of reality to stay there: to be human is to exist, not to be, but to be in place and in time, to operate in the realm of existence, not essence.

2. A Poetics of Particulars

Aristotle takes up Plato's problem at the point where essence takes shape in existence. He avoids universals except in so far as they make themselves known practically in particulars. In particulars, he sees the starting point for poetics. In his hands, poetics becomes exactly what the Greek *poiēsis* would suggest: an analysis of production or making. The question remains how shadows and images communicate reality, but here the question is also how images that communicate reality are made.

The practical problem is how to make representations of persons in action. Following Plato's distinction of simple narrative, imitation, and mixed narrative, Aristotle separates imitation into categories according to the means employed, the models imitated, and the manner in which they are imitated. Imitation is divided into two broad categories: tragedy and comedy. While comedy is said to represent characters worse than average, Aristotle recognizes the fine line between laughter and fear. The object of laughter lacks both self-knowledge and power. The object of fear lacks self-knowledge but possesses power. Tragedy imitates good (complete) action by acting. Actions derive from character or thought. Imitation itself is plot (which is an arrangement of incidents). Character is the basis on which we attribute qualities to agents. Thought is present in everything agents say. Tragedy imitates not persons but complete actions: it imitates wholes—with beginnings, middles, and ends. Aristotle insists on actions that can be perceived as wholes. That which makes no difference by its presence or absence is not part of the whole. Poetry does not describe what has happened but what might happen (that is, possibility). It is closer to philosophy than is history, because it deals with general truths rather than specific events. Yet its specificity is precisely what makes it powerful: because it brings possibility into the realm of existence, it transforms worlds. It makes essence take shape in existence; it makes being be here, now.

Plato's *Republic* explores pragmatics (action) by moving between politics and poetry. Aristotle begins at the end of that progression and, by moving from poetry to pragmatics, casts new light on politics. Both assert a direct connection between politics and ethics, Plato because politics is a macrocosm in which the microcosm of ethics may be clearly examined and Aristotle because politics is a master art that determines the extent to which other arts may be practiced, thereby determining possibilities for good action. This equation makes the movement from politics to poetics to pragmatics an ethically significant one. Good action is qualified and at least partly determined by politics; it is represented by poetry; its representation has an impact on human action. Together, Plato and Aristotle take us full circle—from politics to poetics to pragmatics to politics.

We see human action—complete and incomplete, good and bad—in polity (the city), and we see it in poetry. Polity determines the shape and possibility of human action. Poetry represents that action. Plato saw that poets, who represent human action, are possessors of great power. He also saw that philosophers, in so far as they possess a passion for truth matched by a commitment to seek it (distinct from a compulsion to contain it), are possessors of great power. Aristotle saw that the source of power is a common one: poetry and philosophy are related by birth. Justice depends as much on philosopher-poets as philosopher-rulers. Philosopher-poets must be masters of metaphor; it is such mastery that could make philosopher-rulers.

Aristotle also saw the fine line between fear and laughter, and the connection of both to power. The object of laughter lacks both self-knowledge and power. The object of fear lacks self-knowledge but possesses power. Poets possess power, and philosophers possess self-knowledge. The philosopher-poet, who possesses both, possesses what is necessary to stand against the object of fear. The philosopher-poet lives in the realm of tragedy, the realm of those better than ourselves. Philosophers, poets, and objects of fear live with us, in the world as we know it. Objects of laughter stand in the world of comedy. And yet, that does not reduce comedy to triviality or unimportance. The poet who lacks self-knowledge is an object of fear—one who has power without self-knowledge. The philosopher who lacks power is an object of laughter (as Plato and Aristophanes were aware). The philosopher lifts comedy into our world by possessing a self-knowledge that includes knowledge of his or her own impotence. But this lifting of comedy into the world of existence is the source of power that transforms the philosopher into a philosopher-poet. The object of fear becomes an object of laughter when confronted by knowledge and power; the philosopher-poet renders fear powerless by representing its power as illusion.

Praxis, creative action, is the act of representing illusion. Like the shield of Perseus, it destroys the object of fear by mirroring its destructive power. Like Perseus, its power lies in being aware that the mirror is the secret. And, like Perseus, it needs something outside itself (perhaps the very crone he is afraid of) to give it that awareness.

Kierkegaard wrote of his age (the nineteenth century) that "no age has so fallen victim to the comic." It is

> incomprehensible that this age has not already by a *generatio aequivoca* given birth to its hero, the demon who would remorselessly produce the dreadful spectacle of making the whole age laugh and making it forget that it was laughing at itself. (Kierkegaard, p. 110)

Kierkegaard did not live to see the age that would produce that dreadful spectacle, that *macabre* comedy, and that deadly hero. But we have. The task of the philosopher-poet is, like Socrates, to remind us why we are laughing and what we are laughing at.

The question Plato posed in retrospect as he looked back on the career of Socrates is how to use pieces to picture a whole, how to experience wholeness when all the objects of experience are fragments. Plato found a philosopher who professed to know nothing, then built a city in a poem, an exercise in imagination that condemned those whose medium was the image. Aristotle found an exercise in imagination that professed to be an argument against image-making, then built a theory of image-making that was informed by the action of human beings. We find human beings who act in the middle—of cities, of stories—and whose actions provide the models for images on which cities are built.

Aristotle's definition of tragedy requires wholeness. It becomes comic with the recognition that such wholeness is trapped in fragments. Plot is the heart and soul of tragedy, closely followed by character. It is not individual persons or actions that hold the key to coherence and consistency but the connectedness of actions (plot), the pattern of persons (character). It is pattern and connectedness, the stuff of metaphor. And it is always in question, as Plato noted in terms of justice. The writer of tragedies becomes comic when she or he subsumes the action represented under the universal. Kierkegaard's absolute relation marks it as whole; but, because it is in the middle, it is wholly particular. The poet who forgets this is more frightening than comic if she or he also makes the audience forget.

3. Culture and Nature

Wendell Berry and Joseph Sittler both propose composting as a metaphor for culture. Berry refers to an old bucket hanging on the porch outside his window in which leaves and other organic materials make earth by decaying over a period of years. As surely as this happens in buckets and compost heaps, Berry says, it must happen in human community: "A human community...must collect leaves and stories, and turn them to account. It must build soil, and build that memory of itself...which will be its culture." As culture, building local soil is product and process; but it is more concerned with the collecting than the collected, with the building than the memory built. Berry contends that "if the local culture cannot preserve and improve the local soil, then, as both reason and history inform us, the local community will decay and perish, and the work of soil-building will be resumed by nature." Culture is a subset of nature that operates within a natural process. When it fails, it is engulfed as one more bit of organic matter by that ongoing natural process. Soil is made whether human beings make it or not, but if "a human community...is to last long, [it] must exert a sort of centripetal force, holding local soil and local memory in place. Practically speaking, human society has no work more important than this" (Berry, p. 4). Sittler's image is slightly more interventionist. One must not only gather memory and other organic matter to make soil; one must also regularly stir it up.

Culture is simultaneously concerned with making earth and taking place because it is the interplay of this making and taking that determines whether and where human communities survive. The work of culture is culture. Its primary concern is self-replication, and this process of self-replication is the matrix for human meaning and value. Culture, like other forms of life, emerges out of the tension between order and chaos as a process within nature that runs counter to entropy. The raw material, the material process, and the material product that result from it are all elements of culture. The natural process of making earth acts on all three elements as material. The centripetal force of organization and the centrifugal force of turning (to account, as Berry would have it) both constitute specifically cultural contributions to the process.

The social origins of thought have been the topic of more or less uninterrupted philosophical conversation in the shift from ontology to epistemology that accelerated after Kant. We have already noted some of the consequences of an epistemological turn that marks a return from a world "outside" to a mind "inside." The more constructive turn has been toward sociological epistemology, which Mary Douglas (1986) roots in Ludwik Fleck and Emile Durkheim. She links Fleck's *Denkkollectiv* with the philosophical use of "world" in Nelson Goodman. Like Goodman, she links the question of world to the question of language. Douglas, more than any other contemporary thinker with the possible exception of George Lakoff, has explored the extent to which classifications, logical operations, and guiding metaphors are the social processes through which institutions think and, more importantly, through which they reproduce themselves in the thought and action of individuals. Individuals think through social categories embodied in language and other semiotic systems, but institutions also think through individuals.

This has led a number of writers, including Max Weber and—more recently—Clifford Geertz, to think of human beings as animals suspended in humanly spun webs of significance. Geertz takes culture "to be those webs, and the analysis of it to be therefore not an experimental science in search of law but an interpretive one in search of meaning" (Geertz, p. 5). For Geertz, the definition of culture leads to what Gilbert Ryle calls "thick description." This is description sensitive to multiple contexts and multiple layers of contexts, each of which has an impact on the thing described. You have to sink down into a thing, a matter of weight and of time, to describe it accurately. Thick description abandons isolated things. Because there is no thing except in relationship, webs of significance occupy us (Csikszentmihalyi and Rochberg-Halton, 1981). Thick description "is like trying to read...a manuscript—foreign, faded, full of ellipses, incoherencies, suspicious emendations, and tendentious commentaries, but written not in conventionalized graphs of sound but in transient examples of shaped behavior" (Geertz, p. 10).

Culture is public, a *res publica*, as the Latin designation of Plato's utopian dialogue affirms. Human behavior is symbolic action like "phonation in speech, pigment in painting, line in writing, or sonance in music." As such, it signifies. The point is not to ask what it is but what it does. Geertz writes about the experience in field work of "finding one's feet," an "unnerving business which never more than distantly succeeds" and which always takes time as much as place. Roy Wagner suggests not only that "it might be helpful to think of all human beings, wherever they may be, as 'fieldworkers' of a sort, controlling the culture shock of daily experience through all kinds of imagined and constructed 'rules,' traditions, and fact" (Wagner, 1981, pp. 35-36) but also that this universal process of finding our feet is culture.

The point in field work is not to "become natives" (whatever that might mean) but "to converse with them, a matter a great deal more difficult, and not only with strangers, than is commonly recognized" (Geertz, p. 13). Anthropology's aim, and the aim of thick description in general, is "the enlargement of the universe of human discourse" (Geertz, p. 14). Geertz is aware that anthropology is not the only discipline that pursues this aim, but, he says, it is an aim to which "a semiotic concept of culture is peculiarly well adapted." Culture "is not a power, something to which social events, behaviors, institutions, or processes can be causally attributed; it is a context, something within which they can be intelligibly—that is, thickly—described" (Geertz, p. 14).

It is not culture as context that becomes raw material in Berry's natural process of making earth but the material that remains when the centripetal force of context succumbs to the centrifugal force of entropy.

Geertz maintains that anthropological interpretation "traces the curve of a social discourse" and "fixes it into an inspectable form.... The ethnographer... 'inscribes' social discourse"—writes it down—turning it "from a passing event, which exists only in its own moment of occurrence, into an account, which exists in its inscriptions and can be reconsulted" (Geertz, p. 19). The idea of "inscription" is borrowed from Paul Ricoeur, who asserts that writing "fixes" not the "event" but the "said" of speaking. What we write is "the meaning of the speech event, not the event as event." Cultural analysis is "guessing at meanings, assessing the guesses, and drawing explanatory conclusions from the better guesses, not discovering the Continent of Meaning and mapping out its bodiless landscape" (Geertz, p. 20). It is not a discovery of meaning at all, but a construction (or, as Wagner would say, an invention); and, in that sense it is a making of world such as the one Berry had in mind when he talked about the centripetal force of local culture. Anthropological interpretation, like other cultural products, is an inscription of the kind gathered in the cultural centers—museums, libraries, conservatories, and books—to which Wagner refers.

In anthropology as in other forms of fiction, "explanation often consists of substituting complex pictures for simple ones while striving somehow to retain the persuasive clarity that went with the simple ones" (Geertz, p. 33). Geertz modifies Alfred North Whitehead's maxim for the natural sciences ("seek simplicity and distrust it") to "seek complexity and order it" (p. 34). This simultaneous emphasis on complexity and order is connected to the assertion of modern anthropology that human beings "unmodified by the customs of particular places do not in fact exist, have never existed, and most important, could not in the very nature of the case exist" (Geertz, p. 35). To be human is to be in place, to be modified and to some extent defined by culture. This makes drawing a line "between what is natural, universal, and constant in [humankind] and what is conventional, local, and variable extraordinarily difficult" (Geertz, p. 36). More dramatically, it makes drawing such a line a falsification of the human situation. The drawing of the line is itself conventional, and so natural processes, including reproduction, are culturally defined to the same extent that cultural processes, including the reproduction of culture, are natural.

This could pose serious problems for the value theories discussed in previous chapters. If they depend on a distinction between natural and conventional that can be made only by drawing a line that risks falsification, must we simply abandon the theories with the distinction?

Geertz proposes a transdisciplinary integration of theories and concepts that takes up culture as software, not hardware, which works with the same material

as the natural process within which it is constructed, and treats human beings
as the animals "most desperately dependent upon such extragenetic, outside-the
skin control mechanisms, such cultural programs, for ordering" their behavior
(Geertz, p. 44). Thinking does not consist of "happenings in the head" but of
"traffic in symbols" which, from the point of view of any particular individual,
are "given." They are found when the individual is born, and they remain—with
some modifications—when the individual dies. The individual uses some or all
of them—usually in a spontaneous or unconscious manner, though sometimes
reflectively, "to put a construction upon the events through which he [or she]
lives, to orient himself [or herself] within 'the ongoing course of experienced
things,' to adopt a vivid phrase of John Dewey's" (Geertz, p. 45). They are the
means by which human beings take place and the context, the place, within
which human beings live. Without them, there would be no place to stand, and
we would never find our feet.

This software approach to culture connects it explicitly with the concept of
mind, which Geertz identifies as "neither an action nor a thing, but an organized
system of dispositions which finds its manifestation in some actions and some
things" (p. 58). Geertz conceives human thinking as essentially social, public,
and cultural. Symbols are, as Kenneth Burke suggested, "strategies for
encompassing situations." This directs our attention to how people "define
situations and how they go about coming to terms with them."

The connection of culture with cultivation and with cultural inscription
directs our attention to particular strategies for encompassing situations while
both containing and cultivating arts by which situations are made. Roy Wagner
points to the musical conservatory as a case in point: "it provides a reverent
atmosphere within which the study, practice, recitals, and concerts necessary to
the 'life' of music can be carried on. Cultural institutions not only preserve and
protect the results of [humankind's] refinement, they also sustain it and provide
for its continuation" (Wagner, p. 22).

The placing of cultural inscriptions is itself a construction of a center; the
construction of a center is simultaneously the construction of a matrix; and the
construction of a matrix is simultaneously the construction of value. Charles
Hartshorne's understanding of the aesthetic as the matrix of value that envelopes
the ethical, which in turn envelopes the logical, is instructive. The matrix itself
is judged on aesthetic grounds as a dynamic equilibrium of unity and diversity.
Without diversity, it is of no interest; without unity, it is nothing.

4. Entropy and Art

Writing early in the twentieth century, the Soviet author Yevgeny Zamyatin
(1884-1937) had one of his characters say that children are the only bold

philosophers, remarking the timidity that so often accompanies age. Significantly, the line is woven into a novel called *We*, spoken by a rebellious number in a ruthlessly efficient twenty-sixth century State, yet another variation on the prison in which there is nothing to tell, to another number who, like Zamyatin, is an engineer (Zamyatin, 1993).

Zamyatin wrote the novel in the 1920s, placing it in the context of a post-revolutionary struggle to construct a Soviet State, a struggle that mirrors Plato's imaginative account, between H.G. Wells on one side, Aldous Huxley and George Orwell on the other. Orwell acknowledged Zamyatin's influence, so there is some justification for calling him the "father" of twentieth-century dystopian literature. The label is instructive, joining dysfunction to place (*topos*) and evoking a utopian literary tradition rooted, as I suggested earlier, in Plato, that has relentlessly mapped the territory between no place and good. Zamyatin fathers a critical twentieth-century style that confronts the continuity and connection of depersonalizing places. Though he is routinely co-opted by old anti-Communist cold warriors, a process aided and abetted by his exile to Paris and the troubled history of his novel in Russian, the depersonalizing forces of *We* are bureaucrats, not Bolsheviks. Franz Kafka and Václav Havel are Zamyatin's closest literary cousins. All three confronted bureaucratization that was distinctively Western, as evidenced by Zamyatin's scathing criticism of English society and his references to Frederick Winslow Taylor (1856-1915), an American efficiency expert often referred to as the father of "scientific management," in *We* and elsewhere (Shane, 1968). Taylor's paradoxical influence on Lenin and the formation of the Soviet bureaucracy was noted and criticized by Zamyatin.

We is marked by a fascination with science and technology that is willing to make do with cardboard sets. One advantage of cardboard sets is that they are easily exposed: traveling six centuries into the future, Zamyatin depicts characters flattened in the name of efficiency masquerading as reason. In this possible future, two threats remain: imagination and a mysterious group of people called Mephi who live beyond the walls of the city. As the novel unfolds, a procedure for surgically removing the imagination develops in the background along with a Buck Rogers spacecraft called the Integral, which (despite its name) is intriguingly double. The Integral is a vehicle for traveling beyond every city limit, but it is also a militarily significant means for controlling those who are beyond any city limit.

Zamyatin takes on an old Greek tradition when he depicts the Mephi as primitives; to move beyond the limits of the city is to move back in time, and Mephi who come into the city are vaguely atavistic. Early anthropological literature took up this tradition in its repeated description of every indigenous culture it encountered as primitive. On this note, Zamyatin's fascination with Atilla is intriguing. He did not see the triumph of "the West" and Rome as an advance. Christianity is as good a candidate for comparison to OneState as is the emerging Soviet government; encounter with the Mephi looks a great deal like encounter with pre-Christian, pagan roots (Fletcher, 1997). Zamyatin coyly blurs the boundary: Mephi atavism is in the city as well as out.

Instances of OneState are a dime a dozen in the twentieth century. Retrospectively, the Integral's potential for extending city walls, eliminating what is beyond the limit, focuses attention on totalizing techniques (Herman and Chomsky, 1988). *We* ends with particular brutality (familiar now in Orwellian if not Hitlerian form) when two main characters are destroyed (one physically, the other spiritually) by complicity resulting from surgical removal of the imagination: one suffocates when imagination is removed, then watches approvingly as the other suffocates when air is removed. For Zamyatin, it comes to the same thing: we breathe imagination as surely as we breathe air; an atmosphere devoid of imagination is as lethal as one devoid of oxygen. And coercion is most brutal when it is cloaked in collaboration.

Zamyatin made this explicit in essays that explored the relationship between entropy and art, with reference to the meaning of revolution (Zamyatin, 1991). Zamyatin's revolution is a natural process, the collision of dead, dark stars out of which new stars are born; its law is natural, not social. Zamyatin's Nature includes revolution and entropy. Nothing in Nature is fixed. The philosophical background is Heraclitian rather than Hegelian, significant for interpretation of Marx, who drew on both. It is reminiscent of the image implicit in Berry's old bucket making earth.

That revolution and entropy are equally natural does not render either deterministically necessary. As Zamyatin understood entropy, it means that dissipation of energy is part of every natural process: a hot object cools toward the ambient temperature of a room in which it is placed, just as a cold object warms. Your coffee gets tepid, and your ice cream melts. This march toward tepidity would be inexorable if dead, dark stars did not collide. But they do. And, as a result, the social process of art is not an unrealistic opposition to the necessary process of entropy: it is a necessary process in relation to a world where bright collisions of dark stars are as real as tepid coffee and melted ice cream.

In a social context as obsessed with utility as our own, Zamyatin contrasted "useful" literature in the service of order with "harmful" literature inclined to explode. Harmful literature, paradoxically, is more useful than "useful" literature because it attacks what Zamyatin refers to as congenital sleeping sickness. "Useful" literature is an opiate for a drowsy populace that needs not a sleeping pill but a wake up call.

Chapter Seven

NATURE AND HUMAN NATURE

Mary Wollstonecraft (1759-1797) and Karl Marx stand in a tradition of human rights discourse formed in the eighteenth and nineteenth centuries, profoundly influential in the twentieth, certain to have continuing impact in the twenty-first, associated in each case with an insistent call to wake up. There are obvious and important differences between the two, but the common tradition and its trajectory are worth exploring before turning to specifics, particularly because this trajectory is the context within which Zamyatin's largely neglected understanding of art, entropy, and revolution develops.

Both Wollstonecraft and Marx write in conversation with Edmund Burke (1729-1797), who has come to epitomize organic conservatism in thinking about the legacy of eighteenth and nineteenth-century political philosophy. Wollstonecraft is closely connected with a radical anarchist outlook, though her argument in *A Vindication of the Rights of Woman* does not take that direction. It is striking, in fact, just how conservative—and how organic—each of these thinkers is (in the sense of turning toward and conserving the past, insisting that the future grows through the present out of the past). Marx would be the first to note that to be radical is to go to the root, and it is difficult to get more conservative than that. How much further back can you go than the beginning, how much deeper than the bottom?

Burke's conservatism emerges in reaction to the French Revolution, which dominates political thinking at the turn of the eighteenth century. He had been a supporter of the revolution in the United States but criticized the French for going too far. Wollstonecraft and Marx would argue, on the contrary, that, if anything, they had not gone far enough, the same criticism Zamyatin applied to the Soviet Revolution in the first quarter of the twentieth century, even before Stalin's reactionary regime. The most interesting bit of information contained in this for our present purpose is that all agree that the revolutions were going the same way.

1. The Way of Revolution

The way is crucial. If we are going to understand the debate that hatched at the end of the eighteenth century then exploded in the nineteenth and twentieth, how far is also important.

First, the way. Enlightenment thinking was pretty sanguine about the myth of inevitable progress. In this case, that myth describes a largely European trajectory in which two things happen:

- sovereignty shifts from crown toward people, and
- a body of essential rights, beyond the reach of government, is gradually recognized.

One key to the debate hinges on whether the trajectory is European (as in Wollstonecraft, Paine, and Marx) or English (as in Burke). It is important to keep in mind that, for each of these thinkers, the revolution in the United States is part of the English trajectory. So-called American exceptionalism, which emerges with a vengeance in the nineteenth and twentieth centuries, is an important anomaly that cuts development loose from its roots. But that is a subject for another discussion. This trajectory sees the shift from sovereign, through "virtual" representation, toward republican and parliamentary forms as a healthy human development. In this regard, for Burke, the English parliamentary system is the "end" of history: popular sovereignty—but not too much—and inalienable political rights gradually recognized and negotiated between people and sovereign. Because they are gradually recognized and negotiated, they do not need to be seized or written—certainly not in one fell swoop. And they emerge in a process that looks like a combination of chipping away from below and giving away from above. "Above" and "below," however, are not called into fundamental question—and "higher" powers are expected to put a brake on the excesses of "lower" ones. Burke's criticism of the French Revolution is essentially that the brakes have failed. No wonder he admired the massively redundant braking system built into the institutionally limited revolution in the United States.

A significant portion of Burke's *Reflections on the Revolution in France* is devoted to a response to a 1789 sermon preached by the revolutionary English Unitarian Richard Price (1723-1791). Price unequivocally supported the revolution in France, and he did it with a reference to English history that Burke found particularly threatening. Pointing to the Glorious Revolution of 1688, Price locates the legitimacy of the English sovereign in the will of the people. Burke insists that the legitimacy of any sovereign consists in "a fixed rule of succession according to law." This sets the rule of law in opposition to popular will, only grudgingly granting legitimacy to that will as a temporary basis for sovereignty in times of disorder: "An irregular, convulsive movement may be necessary to throw off an irregular, convulsive disease. But the course of succession is the healthy habit of the British constitution" (Burke, p. 109). Rights are exclusively political, and political rights are primarily procedural.

Enter Wollstonecraft and—later—Marx. Both disagree with Burke on what needs to be braked and what needs to be unleashed.

"Unleashed" is a critical word here in that it suggests an existing but untapped reality. Burke pictures an organic development in which sovereignty, derived from God, rests in a procedure identified with a class represented by one of its members, gradually and grudgingly dispersed to a body politic that grows only as the class in which power resides expands. The body grows as more persons are deemed capable of participating in the exercise of sovereignty. Not surprisingly, the distribution follows a hierarchical pattern reminiscent of Aristotle (except that "barbarians" are now those who do not speak English rather than those who do not speak Greek). The seed of colonial thinking is visible here. Recall that British colonialism was justified for its "civilizing" effect (the "white man's burden") and that independence was granted to British colonies (notably in Africa and the Indian subcontinent) when they were deemed "ready" to exercise it. It is not particularly difficult to locate power in this picture. Burke locates it most explicitly in being British, and this means that, even as sovereignty is gradually dispersed, its locus is law, the "fixed rule of succession" cited above. Whereas Price claims the right of a people to remove its sovereign for misconduct and "to frame a government" for itself, Burke responds that "no government could stand a moment, if it could be blown down with any thing so loose and indefinite as an opinion of 'misconduct'" (Burke, p. 112). Recent experiences with impeachment (in the 1970s and again in the 1990s) in the United States may be taken as evidence of the continuing influence of arguments like the one articulated by Burke.

2. The Language of Rights

The disagreement here is not only over rights, including the right to revolution, but also over the source and desired degree of stability. Zamyatin's indictment of the Soviet Revolution was that it became so concerned with stability that it lost sight of both the possibility and the necessity of change.

In developing a feminist argument, Wollstonecraft intervenes not only in the conversation regarding the French Revolution but also in the hierarchical picture developed by Burke. Most directly, she argues that there is a human nature in which sovereignty is essential rather than derivative. If sovereignty is derived. from God, it rests equally in all human beings, not in a procedure, not in a class, and not in a single individual. Feminism being, as Rebecca West put it, the radical idea that women are people, this means that it belongs to both women and men.

Wollstonecraft makes an interesting and potentially explosive move here. She uses a picture of sovereignty that is radically different from Burke's to launch an attack on an educational system that treats women and men differently, that educates them for different things. This logic will return in U.S. Supreme Court rulings in the twentieth century that slowly and reluctantly recognized that "separate but equal" is not equal. Note that this example raises the question of what is to be braked and what is to be unleashed in another form. The courts in the United States were instrumental beginning in the mid-1950s in bringing Federal power to bear on State and individual abuse of power. Wollstonecraft argues that women and men should be educated for civic participation. In this, she joins contemporaries such as Thomas Jefferson and Thomas Paine. Paine, like Wollstonecraft, was consistent enough to recognize the universality of the claim. If sovereignty belongs to all human beings simply by virtue of our being human, and if education for citizenship is necessary for full participation in the exercise of sovereignty, then all human beings are entitled to such education. And without it, even the best Constitution means nothing.

What is potentially explosive about this claim is that it does not differ dramatically from Burke's proto-colonialism. He can simply claim that women are not "ready" to exercise sovereignty and entrust their education to men. He can also claim (as many have) that "education for citizenship" means nothing more than learning to follow the rules. Jefferson's *Notes on the State of Virginia* seems to confirm this paradox in yet another variation. The same person who could write passionately about inalienable human rights given by "our Creator" could own slaves and speculate (like Aristotle) on their "natural" inferiority. David Walker, who should have a wider audience than he does, called Jefferson to task for this at the same time that he advocated an uprising among Americans of African descent using logic similar to that employed by Jefferson in the U.S. Declaration of Independence. As usual, what we mean by "we" is important.

Apart from the by now obvious insight that this is not easy and that none of the thinkers in question are pure, the most crucial point here is the picture of nature and of civic education that is being sketched. Paine and Walker are no doubt the most consistent thinkers in the group opposed to Burke, though Wollstonecraft is not far behind. The fundamental distinction here is between a world (or a model of the world) in which sovereignty is derivative—from the crown to the people via their representatives—and one in which sovereignty is essential (in the nature of humanity). In the first instance, you have to figure out how to get the powers that be to give you rights and grant you a piece of the pie. In the second, you proclaim that those rights are yours by virtue of being human. There is no need to ask, though there may be a need to demand: hence the revolutions, and, more specifically, the perpetual revolution of the radical Jefferson—and Zamyatin's repeated claim that there is no "final" revolution.

Burke's genealogy of revolution and that of Price both make the "Glorious Revolution" of 1688-1689 pivotal. In that moment, Parliament granted sovereignty to the crown by calling William and Mary to share the throne. Some of this had been played out in Church history the century before with Reformation debates regarding the relative authority of Councils, Scripture, and the Pope. Parliament represented the people, and, in Price's view, this act confirmed its superiority over the crown. The revolution in the United States continued this process, solidifying a representative government shielded from the passions of direct popular sovereignty (the Senate playing a role parallel to the House of Lords in the British Parliament and the Electoral College assuring that—in spite of repeated claims to the contrary—the President is not simply elected by "all the people"). Burke disagrees with Price regarding the superiority of the people over the crown, but he could approve the process because it clarifies and limits the idea of virtual representation by spelling out who can represent whom. A close reading of the U.S. Constitution will confirm that lots of folks (notably slaves, Indians, and women) were formally excluded; but Burke, Jefferson, and John Adams each claimed in his own way that this was done in the best interest of the excluded. Burke in particular locates this "best interest" in restoration of order where order has been disrupted and preservation of order where it has not.

When the French Revolution broadened the sphere of representation and discarded rules of succession, Burke judged that it had crossed a line. Marx returned to consider this half a century later.

As we have noted before, Marx located our human nature in our work: we are human to the extent that we transform the world of nature into a world of culture. That, we noted earlier, is the source of value; but here we can also say that it is the locus of power and sovereignty. We "exercise dominion" over Nature in the act of transforming it into culture. It is not surprising, then, that Marx's politics develops along lines that put workers on the vanguard. Nor is it surprising that he speaks (in a stridently utopian tone) of the withering away of the State. If work is what makes us human, then we will all be "on the vanguard" in a fully human world. In the meantime, there is a "dictatorship of the proletariat" and a "revolutionary" vanguard consisting of loyal members of the Party. The tendency of both toward hierarchy, elitism, and brutality are well known. As a practical interpreter of Marx, Lenin was every bit as contradictory as Jefferson.

My reference at the beginning of this chapter to the "organic" ground shared by Burke, Wollstonecraft, and Marx bears repeating; it is best understood in the light of Zamyatin's equally organic image, cited at the end of the last chapter. Burke's fears focused on the revolutionary dissolution of the body politic within which he lived: centrifugal forces associated with popular sovereignty threatened to dismember the body. Wollstonecraft, Marx, and Zamyatin focused on a body in danger of suffocating under its own weight. Marx, writing from ground zero of the industrial revolution, could connect this (as he did especially in his 1844

Manuscripts) with the mechanization of human workers. Zamyatin witnessed the curious hybridization of Marx and Taylor (in England as much as in the Soviet Union) that threatened to mechanize human society. The danger was not so much that the body would be dismembered as that it would be incorporated into a ruthlessly efficient machine—a chillingly accurate description from our vantage point on the far side of the twentieth century.

In terms of rights talk, this raises a number of critical questions that we can take to a succession of twentieth century documents against an eighteenth century background:

- Are some rights "natural"—ours simply by virtue of our humanity?
- If so, how are those rights protected, and who must recognize them?
- Are there other rights that are "cultural," "economic," "political," or "social"?
- If so, who grants those rights, how are they protected, and who must recognize them?
- If there is a distinction among types of rights, what is the significance both of keeping them distinct and of confusing them?

The movement from the Declaration of the Rights of Man and the Citizen (late eighteenth century) through the Universal Declaration of Human Rights and the Freedom Charter (mid-twentieth century) to the South African Constitution (late twentieth century) is a narrative in which rights talk that began with strictly limited political and social discourse moves increasingly toward cultural and economic discourse. The South African Constitution, for example, devotes significant space to language and religion (in ways that bear comparison to the much more tentative treatment of those matters in the U.S. Constitution). The Freedom Charter devotes significant attention to land (as did Radical Reconstructionists in the second phase of the U.S. revolution after the Civil War in the United States). The Universal Declaration of Human Rights strongly suggests that cultural and economic rights should have a status equivalent to that of civil and political rights.

Expanding the field of discourse about rights does not necessarily address Zamyatin's concern, or that of Wollstonecraft. But it may open a space within which to reconsider questions of civic virtue without shutting down human vulnerability or suppressing explosive stories.

Chapter Eight

CULTIVATING RULES

In *Foundations of the Metaphysics of Morals*, published in 1785, Immanuel Kant locates himself with reference to an ancient Greek division of philosophy into physics, ethics, and logic. This is a distinction between formal philosophy (logic) and material philosophy (physics and ethics). Material philosophy is further divided according to whether its matter is nature or freedom. The matter of ethics is freedom. Both branches of material philosophy include empirical and rational aspects. In ethics, the empirical is practical anthropology, while the rational is moral philosophy. The rational aspect of the branch of material philosophy whose matter is freedom concerns Kant in this work, so he begins with a distinction between practical rules (the concern of anthropology) and moral laws (the concern of philosophy).

Ethics consists of empirical and rational aspects, but the metaphysics of Kant's title singles out the rational. Kant inherited Leibnizian rationalism via Christian Wolff and encountered British empiricism carried to its skeptical extreme in David Hume. Hume's empiricism is a limit, encountered as one might encounter another human being with whom one collides, and Kant's mature philosophical enterprise consists in the construction of a language with which to carry forward a fundamentally rationalist discipline constrained by empirical limits.

This is a significant point of comparison with Piaget and Marx, both of whom owe a great deal to Kant. Both Marx and Piaget sought to establish a dialectical unity between theory and practice, reason and experience. Marx spoke of the senses becoming theoreticians in practice, and Piaget's genetic epistemology described a practice by which knowledge is constructed. For Kant, emphasis on moral laws detached from practical rules meant a focus on duty that, given the imperfection of human will and the limits of human reason, becomes a focus on imperative. His foundation of ethical theory distinguishes between categorical and hypothetical imperatives. Like Piaget's teleonomic processes, Kant's ethic tends in theory toward necessity.

1. Practical Reason

Kant states three propositions of morality:

- First, to have moral worth, an action must be done from duty.

- Second, an action performed from duty does not have its moral worth in the purpose to be achieved but in the maxim by which it is determined.
- Third, duty is the necessity of an action executed from respect for law.

These propositions shift attention from discrete actions toward laws by which they are connected and in which their necessity is grounded. In Kant's theory of ethics, it is not the action but the maxim of the action that is important. This leads to his first statement of the categorical imperative: "I should never act in such a way that I could not also will that my maxim should be a universal law" (Kant, p. 18). Will is connected with law not by way of action but by way of the maxim of action. Because the maxim of an action is revealed in the action—the practice, will is equated with practical reason. Kant's fully developed ethic is thus a critique of practical reason, as distinct from a critique of pure reason.

The distinction between categorical and hypothetical imperatives is a variation on the distinction between deontological and teleological ethics. A hypothetical imperative is a maxim that locates the necessity of an action in some end outside the action itself: one must do x in order to accomplish y. It is hypothetical—in the sense of conditional—because if one does x, then y will be accomplished. A categorical imperative presents the action itself as objectively necessary, without regard to any other end: one must do x.

An equally important distinction between autonomy and heteronomy follows, one that is crucial for theories of moral development derived from Piaget. Hypothetical imperatives require teleological ethics and are by definition heteronomous. The necessity of their laws (*nomos*) always resides in an other (*heteros*), and the other becomes an end (*telos*) to which duty is subordinated. Categorical imperatives require deontological ethics and demand autonomy. The necessity of their laws always resides in the action itself and the will is brought into conformity with the imperative in the self (*autos*) that acts.

This explains another variation of the categorical imperative, that human beings are always to be treated as ends in themselves, never as means. In the realm of ends, Kant maintains, everything has a price or a dignity. In language that anticipates Marx, he notes that what is related to human inclinations and needs has a market price and that its value is equivalent to this price. That which constitutes the condition under which something can alone be an end in itself has no price: it is a dignity. From a Marxist perspective, this may be taken to suggest that teleological ethics determine the worth of human actions with reference to ends whose values are determined by the market. Under such a scheme, what has no price might easily come to be defined not as priceless but as worthless.

Kant's foundation of ethical theory examines duty and imperative to focus attention on law and will. The critical language in which the foundation is articulated distinguishes ends and means and poses two questions that are crucial for the discipline of ethics: the other and the self. If law is to be located in self, then understanding this self *vis-à-vis* other is at least as important for ethics as understanding law.

2. Moral Development

That ethics is as concerned with understanding self and relationship as with understanding law directs our attention to the development of self in relationship already suggested in the brief reference above to theories of moral development derived from Piaget. The best known of these theories, associated with Lawrence Kohlberg and Carol Gilligan, have a great deal in common—though this should not be allowed to obscure important differences. Kohlberg set out to expand on Piaget's groundbreaking work (in *The Moral Judgment of the Child*), and Gilligan set out to correct flaws resulting from Kohlberg's limited sample.

Piaget begins with the observation that knowing develops out of action across time. This is why he called himself a genetic epistemologist rather than a psychologist: his concern was with the genesis of knowing. This means that knowledge cannot be treated as a static thing, nor can its development be understood simply as a process of accumulation. Applied to ethics, it means that moral judgment—like other forms of knowing—is an active process that develops across time.

Approaching this on an individual level, we would expect to see a transformation of moral judgment as the individual grows from childhood to adulthood. Keeping the transformation connected to action means that it is not simply a maturation process. Obviously, we change in some necessary ways as we get older—regardless of what we do. But Piaget is a good Kantian here: freedom is the matter of ethics, so we attend not to what happens regardless of what we do or what happens as a result of what we do but to what we do. We have talked about the structure of action itself before, and we return to it here.

Piaget isolated a structure of action that could be observed genetically— across time: a game. Observing children in Geneva playing marbles, he noted a systematic transformation of thinking about rules that appeared to be present both in individual children as they got older and in comparisons of children at different points in their cognitive development. He spotted a pattern.

In very general terms, the earliest interaction between children and marbles was more or less random—not rule-governed at all. A young child might pick up a marble, drop it into a bunch of other marbles, and laugh when the bunch scattered. The youngest children would probably pop the marble into their mouths, a biologically significant fact of which Piaget was aware but that would divert our attention here. The repetition of this act is the earliest form of rule, which suggests a connection between rule and repetitive action. Notice that it also suggests a connection between repetitive action and predictable (or expectable) results. If the marbles did not scatter, the child might reassess his or her action.

Put two or more young children together with a bunch of marbles, and their repetitive actions begin to interact in ways that might well precipitate such reassessment. The young child who has learned to scatter a bunch of marbles by dropping a single marble loses control of the scattering if there is another child dropping marbles. One way to regain control is to institute rules as regulators of action—taking turns, for example.

Complete control would ruin the game. The child who laughs when the marbles scatter is likely to get bored if they always do the same thing—as is a group of children whose individual actions no longer have any clear connection to the movement of the marbles. It might be a lot of fun to just scatter the marbles wildly all over the place, but that activity ends in boredom (or lost marbles) as well.

Piaget noticed that rules regulated social interaction in the game of marbles in ways that facilitated social (as opposed to individual) control and individual participation without eliminating surprise. This is important in terms of understanding the genesis of the self as well as the genesis of rules. Where is the self located?

The game of marbles is not spontaneously invented every time children come together. It is an old game, with established rules. In Geneva, this generally meant that older children taught the game to younger ones, a fact that was important in Vygotsky's early criticism of Piaget and in Piaget's subsequent modification of his own theories. One of the most interesting questions about the rules of an old game is how young children come to know them. In Geneva, older children did not tell younger children the rules so much as they showed them in practice. Young children learn the rules of the game by playing the game.

As I said earlier, Piaget spotted a pattern: from random action, to conscious (observed) action, to repetitive action, to social interaction, to regulated social interaction.

Young children who had just learned the game often saw the rules as imposed from outside—made up in one famous line by "an old gentleman in Geneva." Experienced (generally, but not necessarily, older) players developed a consciousness of the regulative function of the rules by observation. This meant that they came to a point at which they recognized the rules not as arbitrarily imposed but as socially constructed: the game depends on observation of the rules, but groups could agree to change them at any time. To the sequence above, then, add another step: conscious (observed) regulated social interaction.

Another way to describe this is as a movement from arbitrary action through externally regulated action to internally regulated action. Notice that "internal" here is internal to a group, not simply to an individual.

Piaget generalized from this observation of a small localized sample to a global claim about human development, and he has been criticized for overgeneralizing. That is a legitimate criticism that most certainly should be tested.

Kohlberg elaborated this observation of rules into a more comprehensive theory of moral development. He contended that moral development necessarily followed the pattern described by Piaget—by which he meant most specifically the movement from arbitrary action, through externally regulated action, to internally regulated action. In Kohlberg's theory, this was described as three levels of moral thinking: preconventional, conventional, and post-conventional. Kohlberg combined this descriptive framework with motivational theory and suggested that the movement from preconventional to conventional behavior is fueled by a succession of rewards. The most basic is "instrumental hedonism," satisfaction of instinctual needs. Beyond that is a need for the approval of others who have power to satisfy needs. For Kohlberg, then, moral development moves from instrumental hedonism toward a "good boy-good girl" orientation, then toward a "law and order" orientation. He suggested that this "conventional" level is as far as most adults get in moral development, meaning that moral behavior can generally be described in culturally specific conventional terms.

But he did describe a "post-conventional" level reached by fewer adults in which moral behavior is regulated by principles, the highest of which is justice. According to Kohlberg, moral agents at this level resolve dilemmas in which conventions come into conflict with principles by choosing principle over rule. This is exemplified by Augustine's claim (taken up by Martin Luther King, Jr.) that "an unjust law is no law."

Kohlberg laid out a moral developmental scale (consisting of three levels, each divided into two stages) on which persons could be placed based on their responses to a series of moral dilemma stories.

Carol Gilligan was a student of Kohlberg at Harvard who noted, first, that Kohlberg's theory was based on study of adolescent boys and, second, that adolescent girls tended to score lower than boys on the moral developmental scale. This suggested a problem with the scale, not the girls. So Gilligan reassessed the theory.

She noticed that girls confronted with moral dilemmas tended to approach them not as conflicts between rules and principles but as problems in relationships. Accepting the basic framework articulated by Piaget and expanded by Kohlberg, she suggested that moral development proceeded along two dimensions, one identified as a "justice" orientation, the other as an orientation of "care." A "justice" orientation is probably close to what Aristotle had in mind when he said "I love my friends, but I love the truth more." A "care" orientation would dismiss this as a false dichotomy.

It is important to bear in mind that Gilligan does not make a biological claim here about some essential sexual difference between males and females. She makes a social-cultural claim about ways in which gender has been socially constructed. In her view, full human development involves an embrace of both "justice" and "care" orientations—an embrace that involves rethinking ways in which gender is constructed in society.

For our purposes, this serves as yet another variation on the theme of the good city. But it also directs our attention to a tendency to set up a dichotomy between freedom and rule. Piagetian theories of moral development, exemplified in Gilligan's work, join Kant in approaching freedom as the matter of ethics—and they do not expect to find this matter excluded in rule.

Kant's categorical imperative at its best is a way of formulating rule as a foundation for freedom rather than an impediment: free action is not action against categorical imperatives, though it may shatter hypothetical ones. Gilligan expands on this by focusing on the connection between rule and relationship. It is in relationship—the collision with *other* as undeniable concrete necessity—that rule originates. What, we might ask Aristotle, is truth apart from friends—and where shall we expect to find it if not between friends?

Chapter Nine

RULE AND RELATIONSHIP

Tragic drama capitalizes on the common knowledge that people are routinely ruined by things that "just happen," and that good people often do bad things because of circumstances beyond their control. As Martha Nussbaum notes, however, Aeschylean tragedy dwells on uncommon situations in which a good person does a bad thing in full knowledge of its nature. Moral philosophy since Socrates has attacked the logical inconsistency of that dwelling, preferring a Sophoclean vision; but Nussbaum argues that it reflects our practical intuitions in situations of ordinary conflict better than the theories that label it primitive (Nussbaum, pp. 25-26).

1. The Soul of Tragedy

Aeschylus (525-456 BCE) begins his *Agamemnon* with an omen, an ominous intersection of heaven and earth: in a pregnant moment, two eagles devour a pregnant hare. Nussbaum reads this in the light of Agamemnon's sacrifice of his daughter, Iphigenia. The chorus sees the sacrifice as necessary but holds Agamemnon responsible. In this case, necessity is the result of a contingent intersection of two divine commands: Zeus places a guilt-free person where there is no guilt-free path. Agamemnon responds by making himself a willing collaborator, "arranging his feelings to accord with his fortune" (Nussbaum, p. 35), and the chorus holds him responsible for his inference from the necessity of the sacrifice to its rightness. Though Nussbaum distinguishes this sacrifice from Abraham's sacrifice of Isaac—or Ismael, in the Qur'anic version, the sacrifices have in common the willful bringing of human will into conformity with the will of the divine. It is interesting in this regard that Euripides would later include a similar confluence in Polyxena, a character in his *Hecuba* whose fate contributes to the disintegration of Hecuba's character in the play. Faced with a sentence of death as unjust as the one imposed on Isaac or Ismael, Polyxena does not implore Odysseus to spare her. She wishes to do what she must do: will and duty coalesce (348-351).

  The Greek proverb *ta de moi pathemata mathemata gegone* ("what I have suffered has become knowledge") does not mean simply that "through the means of suffering (experience) comes (intellectual) understanding" but also that each "passional reaction" is a piece of "practical perception" (Nussbaum, p. 45). Agamemnon's arrangement of his feelings to accord with his fortune makes him morally culpable in the sacrifice of his daughter, but it is also an instance of practical perception structured by passional reaction. Nussbaum suggests that such perception is not necessarily reactive; it may also structure life to avoid the kind of conflict Agamemnon faced—to simplify moral commitments. In this regard, the more striking Hebrew parallel to Agamemnon's sacrifice is the sacrifice of Jephthah's daughter described in Judges 11. In Jephthah's simplified moral universe, keeping a vow rashly made takes precedence over sustaining relationship with one's child. Jephthah, like Agamemnon, has been judged culpable even by many who have read his act as a necessary outcome of his vow. Jephthah's unnamed daughter, like Ismael and Polyxena, willingly submits to an arbitrary death sentence, not only rearranging her feelings to accord with her fortune but also perceiving the world as one in which passion is a perfectly natural product of fortune, a necessary foundation for free action. Whether these stories are read as tragedies, as moral exemplars, as texts of terror, or as all three has been an important starting point for ethical reflection on the complexity of both extraordinary and ordinary conflict (Reineke, 1997; Trible, 1984).

Nussbaum points to the *Antigone* of Sophocles (495-406 BCE) as an account of two attempts at the kind of moral simplification to which she refers. The play begins with a guard who arrives dragging his feet, a picture of ordinary deliberation simply but vividly drawn to highlight the extent to which Antigone and Creon have removed themselves from the ordinary. Because Creon equates reason with devotion to the city, he sees Antigone's challenge to civil law as plainly and simply irrational. The familial relationship that joins Creon to Antigone leads the audience to expect painful tension, but what we see initially is a relatively painless resolution. We get the tension we expect between characters, but not, in the beginning, within them. Creon's equation of "good" with "good for the city" and "bad" with "bad for the city," along with his similarly circumscribed view of justice, makes Antigone's violation of civil law easy for him to categorize and contain.

While Creon centers on the city and draws a line between invading and defending forces, Antigone draws a circle around her family. But she is not motivated by particularity in her relationship to Haemon or Ismene. Nussbaum cites Ismene's characterization: she has "a warm heart for the cold" (Nussbaum, p. 64). For Antigone, duty to the family dead—and, more particularly, keeping the dead in their place—is the supreme law, as surely as civic duty—and more particularly, keeping the living in their place—is the supreme law for Creon. One maintains a society of the dead, the other a society of the living; but both see the maintenance primarily as a matter of ritual observance rather than human interaction. Both Antigone and Creon set themselves up as arbiters of what the gods can and cannot decree. Nussbaum sees the two characters as complementary, not contradictory: while Creon's attitude is necrophilic, Antigone's is a desire to be a *nekros*, a corpse (Nussbaum, p. 65). Neither Creon nor Antigone is drawn by Sophocles as a loving or passionate character: both are cold, and both seek to protect a structure—city or family—by freezing it in place. In Nussbaum's reading, however, both finally retract their ruthlessly simplifying theories of practical reason under the pressure of complex events and relationships. Part of the interest of the play is its development of the expected tension within characters from tension between characters. Like Aeschylus, Sophocles is interested in the complex causal relationship between a tragic universe and the characters that inhabit it, and the construction of those characters takes the form of relentless complication in the face of a variety of strategies for simplification. The Sophoclean soul is like Heraclitus's "spider sitting in the middle of its web, able to feel and respond to any tug in any part of the complicated structure." This soul "advances its understanding of life and of itself not by a Platonic movement from the particular to the universal, from the perceived world to a simpler, clearer world, but by hovering in thought and imagination around the enigmatic complexities of the seen particular..." Correct choice is a matter of "keenness and flexibility of perception, rather than of conformity to a set of simplifying principles" (Nussbaum, p. 69).

Polynices's corpse embodies a tension between the complexity of a war in which members of a single family fight on opposite sides and the simplicity of Creon's edict. The eye of nature sees complexity where Creon's eye sees simplicity. The eyes of the audience see the complexity of these contrasting visions. Creon's "strange eye" stands in contrast to the eye of the sun, which embraces conflict and complexity; the eyes of the chorus, which are receptive, not active and controlling; and the eyes of an audience in a position of open waiting, willing "to be surprised and moved, in company with others." By the time Antigone is entombed, the play has constricted from sunshine to a cave. The ode at her entombment pictures a world in which all humans are yoked like animals (944-987). Nussbaum reads the end as a tension between "active harmonizing" and "open responsiveness" and tentatively sides with Schopenhauer against Hegel: a sense of paralysis is the proper response to tragedy.

But *Antigone* does not end with paralysis: a blind man—Tiresias—enters, led by a child. From this "community of response, comes the possibility of action" (Nussbaum, p. 79). Tiresias, a priest of Apollo, a god associated with ordering and bounding, urges Creon to heal himself of the rage for control, a sickness common to all human beings. The cure is good deliberation—connected with yielding, renunciation of self-willed stubbornness, and flexibility. The image of learning proposed by Tiresias and Haemon is not the opposite of Creon's active control—they do not tell him to become passive and inert. They counsel flexible responsiveness—a practical wisdom "that bends responsively to the shape of the natural world." Flexibility is not only more prudent than rigidity but also more beautiful and hence more "civilized."

Euripides's *Hecuba*—to which I have already briefly referred—has, as
Nussbaum argues, much in common with Aristotle and Protagoras. Hecuba
maintains that ethical values are human and cannot be treated lightly. If morality
is a system of human practices, there is a distinct possibility that human
circumstances can defile *nomoi*. That *nomos* is not simply "out there" means that
there is nowhere to turn in times of upheaval. If openness is a central element
of noble character, then the breakdown of trust can shatter the nobility of the
noblest character (Nussbaum, pp. 403-405). The murder of her son Polydorus
brings about an abrupt change in Hecuba's character. Polymestor is described as
both *xenos* ("guest-friend") and *philos* ("loved one") of Hecuba and Priam.
Because there is a sacred bond of hospitality and affection between them,
Polymestor's crime is a worst case. Hecuba is an extreme case of adult excellence
that mirrors Polymestor's extreme case of crime: if Hecuba can fall, anybody
can; and if anything can make her fall, it is a crime like the one Polymestor
commits (Nussbaum, pp. 406-407).

The servant who brings Polydorus's body sees the news as a blasphemy
against everything. Hecuba sees that the deepest trustworthiness is not
trustworthy. It is a dislocation—nobody, Hecuba says, is more in disorder than
she, except Disorder herself. This external betrayal, outside her control, is a
defilement of her character. She must either blind herself and be a fool or open
her eyes and be contaminated. At this point, Euripides has already examined the
transformation of Hecuba from queen to slave, defining slavery in the voice of
Coryphaeus (332-334): "to be abused and bear it, compelled by violence to suffer
wrong." At the moment of that transformation, depicted in the *Trojan Women*,
the "sane" Hecuba counsels submission, while the "mad" Cassandra calls for
resistance. When the deepest trustworthiness is proved untrustworthy, Hecuba
joins the mad Cassandra; but she never ceases to connect suffering with wisdom.
Euripides focuses on the new music (*nomos*) of Hecuba's shattered world:
shattering is not only unstructuring but also restructuring. Revenge is the *nomos*
that fills the place left by the collapse of the old. Revenge attracts in this case
because it promises structure and plan without vulnerability (Nussbaum, pp.
407-409), strikingly parallel to the course of the war depicted by Euripides.

Nussbaum maintains that there are both retributive and mimetic aspects of
Hecuba's revenge. Her plan claims to imitate the world as it always was. It was
never trustworthy, and Hecuba concludes that she was deluded to have believed
it so. Her blinding of Polymestor is retributive, but it also brings to light what
was always the case. Hers is more a refusal to see than to be seen, and this is a
revelation of the depth of the affection Polymestor has betrayed. Because she is
what he sees when he sees her, she now knows that this would make her
nothing. She must resist the old *nomos* in order to secure a new one (Nussbaum,
pp. 409-413). Hecuba "makes the world over in the image of the possibility of
non-relation" (Nussbaum, p. 413). Revenge transforms what had been Hecuba's

highest values into mere means. The shell of character remains: it is nobility that is missing. Language changes, too, becoming untrustworthy, though Hecuba would now claim that it had always been so (Nussbaum, pp. 415-416). For Euripides, what had always been so is both an interweaving of hope with fear and a smothering of hope under accumulating layers of fear: the fear of the Greeks and the fear of Polymestor murder Hecuba's hope. Polymestor's reason for murdering Polydorus (1135-1145) echoes the Greeks' reason for murdering Astyanax: the Greeks fear a second Troy, and Polymestor fears that a second Troy founded by Polydorus would bring down the wrath of the Greeks. Polydorus dies for fear of fear, and Hecuba is undone.

In *Oresteia*, Aeschylus showed us the foundation of the city as the replacement of revenge structures with structures of civic trust and civic friendship (Nussbaum, p. 410), language also used by Václav Havel before, during, and after his country's "velvet revolution." In *Hecuba*, Euripides inverts the process to demonstrate that our self-creation as political beings is not irreversible. Not only in *Hecuba*, but also in *Andromache*, *Helen*, and the *Trojan Women*, Euripides experiments with the transformation of character, particularly as it relates to the disintegration of civic trust that is an unavoidable byproduct of war. The *Trojan Women* depicts the destruction of Troy as a simultaneous barbarization of the Greeks, distilling these parallel histories in the particular murder of Hector and Andromache's son. Andromache relinquishes Astyanax to the Greeks when she is reluctantly ordered to do so by Talthybius, but she curses their cleverness as "simple barbarity" (709-779). When Talthybius returns Astyanax's body to Hecuba on Hector's shield (1018-1206), she rages at the Greeks for being afraid of a baby and repeats a familiar theme of Euripidean tragedy: "That mortal is a fool who, prospering, thinks his life has any strong foundation; since our fortune's course and action is the reeling way a madman takes, and no one person is ever happy all the time (1203-1205)." Euripides's depiction of this war echoes Andromache's cry (385): "If I win, I lose; And losing, losing—oh, I'm lost forever!" The human being is the being that can most easily cease to be itself—becoming either god or dog, both movements that involve a loss of human value. If we were not changeable for better and worse, we would not be human. We do not gain purity or simplicity without losing richness and fulness. This changeability is our humanity, both hope and curse, articulated by Andromache near the beginning of the play that bears her name (100) and repeated with variations throughout the body of Greek tragedy: "It's vain to say that any man alive is in the true sense happy. Wait and ponder the manner of his exit from the stage."

2. The Temptation of Knowledge

Emmanuel Levinas begins with *Talmud*, a written transcription of oral tradition marked by "oceanic rhythm," a reading of *Torah* in search of problems and truths (Levinas, p. 9). He sets himself the task of "translating" this reading—and this rhythm—into Greek, into the language of Europe. But he does not so much convey *Talmud* to Europe (it has, after all, been there a long time already) as include Europe in its oceanic rhythm.

Levinas looks to *praxis*, not word, for signification about God. And he takes up the image of intersection and conjunction in a "dialectic of the collective and the intimate" (p. 17) that always carries risk: "as soon as two are involved, everything is in danger" (p. 14). But note that *praxis* does not exclude word: "speech, in its original essence, is a commitment to a third party on behalf of our neighbor: the act *par excellence*, the institution of society." Responsibility is the essence of language (Levinas, p. 20), and it bridges any perceived gap between what is written and what is spoken. This text, though written, is an oral tradition.

Talmud requires discourse and companionship, which are thoroughly entangled with forgiveness. Vengeance and retaliatory justice cannot be denied to those wronged—but to "be Israel" is not to claim this right (Levinas, p. 28). The story of Rizpah Bat Aiah (2 Samuel 21) stands side by side with Antigone, reminders that there is no heart without reason, no reason without heart (Levinas, p. 27). David learns that a three year famine is the result of Saul's actions against the Gibeonites, which Levinas later describes as depriving them of their means of subsistence. He sends for the Gibeonites and listens to their grievances. They have nothing against the Children of Israel but want seven of Saul's descendants whom they intend to nail to a rock. David takes two sons from Rizpah (Saul's concubine) and five from Michal (Saul's daughter) and hands them over to the Gibeonites, who execute them as promised. But Rizpah stays with the corpses from Passover to Succoth, covering them each evening with bags to protect them from birds and other animals. What remains, Levinas says, "after so much blood and tears shed in the name of immortal principles is individual sacrifice." But attending to the human does not exclude the divine, which we encounter at crossroads of human journeyings (Levinas, p. 32).

The temptation of knowledge "is to be simultaneously outside everything and participating in everything" (Levinas, p. 34). This looks like the version of Platonic philosophy criticized by Nussbaum, the subordination of act to the knowledge that one may have of that act (Levinas, p. 35). In this version, "spontaneous engagement, in contrast to a theoretical exploration which should, in principle, precede it, is either impossible and dangerous, or provisional" (Levinas, p. 35). But the provisional character, reminiscent of what Creon gradually learns, suggests that "the notion of action, instead of indicating *praxis* as opposed to contemplation, a move in the dark, leads us to an order in which the opposition of engagement and disengagement is no longer decisive and which precedes, even conditions, these actions" (Levinas, p. 36).

Freedom begins in what appears to be restraint (Levinas, p. 40), and "Reason, *once it comes into being*, includes its pre-history" (Levinas, p. 38). The image cultivated by Levinas looks as Heraclitean as that embraced by Nussbaum: a spider and her web, sensitive to every movement in every part in every direction.

As in Nussbaum's reading of Aristotle, the Universal is vanquished by the local (Levinas, p. 66). Here it has profound implications for "promised" lands: "even an absolutely moral people would have no right to conquest" (Levinas, p. 67).

The city of Levinas is an assembly of faces, not a joint stock company, an open circle (p. 72) which needs the other—every other—to increase the twenty three to seventy one. Levinas imagines a case before one of the two Sanhedrins of twenty three judges on which the life of a man depends. Twelve vote for death, eleven against. The law does not permit a death sentence on the basis of a one vote majority. The twenty three judges are seated in a semi-circle; students of the law are seated before them by rank. The two highest students are asked to join the judges, increasing their number to twenty five. The case is argued again, and the vote is thirteen to twelve. The process is repeated and can go on until the court is increased to seventy one judges, the number of the great Sanhedrin. Since everyone moves up one seat with each iteration, the most competent members of the public are called to fill the empty places created at the end, when all the students have moved up. The Sanhedrin of twenty three is transformed into the great Sanhedrin; students of the law are transformed into judges; and members of the public are transformed into students of the law—all this "at the navel of the world" (Levinas, p. 74). There can be, he says, no masses; every one must be part of the elite (p. 81).

Levinas insists on the necessity of a community which carries out the *mitzvot* right here and now (p. 83). In every moment, we are responsible for others, hostage to others (p. 85). Morality starts with "the man who is hostage to all others" (p. 87). One moves, all move: not a contingent, but an absolute distribution (p. 87), an embrace of the universe, an escape not from but toward danger (p. 192).

Gerald Bruns associates Nussbaum with analytic, Levinas with continental theory. The former, he says, concerns itself with beliefs, desires, values, principles, perceptions, actions, and experiences; the latter concerns itself with "how we are with respect to other people." Nussbaum has given up framing ethics in terms of rules and beliefs but still conceives it in terms of a moral spectator (Bruns, p. 208). Levinas, on the other hand, conceives ethics as a relationship between myself and the stranger over whom I have no power (Bruns, p. 209).

The distinction is too sharply drawn: Nussbaum's "Greek" theory is tragic while Levinas's "Jewish" theory is comic. Both embrace the poetic task described by Bruns: "not so much to know as to abide with reality," to learn to "inhabit" it (p. 212).

Here, John Cage is helpful for ethics. His attention to listening to the world, to letting sound be sound, his evocation of the circus as a new form of living together, his embrace of a structure of greater complexity, is a contribution to "minding" the world—not "caring" for it but being fully present to it, writing on water, composing a musical body "in which the free play of differences are given vent and let be without interference" (Bruns, p. 191).

A story is an intersection in which all lines cross. There are those who regard the stories with which Cage's compositions and conversations were peppered as diversions. Perhaps. But only if diversion lies at the heart of artistic composition, where these stories lie.

"We need a plan," Cage said, "that leaves us free to do what we are capable of doing." That, I believe, is equivalent to his often repeated claim that art equals "imitation of nature in her manner of operation" (*Biology and the History of the Future*, 1972). Not holding up a mirror to nature, but doing what nature does, which is all we can do, because we are the body in which nature does it.

Chapter Ten

CONFESSION AND COMMUNITY

Confession is inextricably connected with trial, an image that includes both public testimony and acknowledgment of sin. As public testimony, it implies the existence of an audience that extends beyond the boundaries of the confessing individual or community; it poses the problem of communication. As acknowledgment of sin, it implies the existence of boundaries or limits that have been overstepped; it poses the problem of relationship. Both implications affirm the existence of an other over against whom one's self or one's community is defined and with whom one stands in relationship.

That one stands in relationship is intrinsically connected with limit as well as with communication. *Peras* is joined with *mythos*; myth crosses boundaries to transform confrontation into communication.

1. *Status Confessionis*

Status evokes an image of place. It is the structured space within which one lives and breathes. It is at once a position within a particular context, usually a hierarchically ordered one, and the context within which one lives. As "state," it circumscribes repertoires of action and response; it shapes roles and may be defined by the roles to which it gives birth.

The particular circumscription of action known as "trial" is a *status* that gives rise to testimony: it is a state that necessitates confession. A *status confessionis* is a situation in life analogous to trial. The structure of existence calls the very meaning of existence into question. This implies that *status* and confession are mutually transformative. The *status* necessitates the confession; it is also the context within which confession emerges and takes shape. But the confession that emerges is itself transformative: it reshapes the *status* within which and from which it emerges.

To describe a *status* as the context within which confession emerges and takes shape as well as the necessity that lies behind the confession itself is to suggest a connection between action and passion. This is reminiscent of the Greek proverb cited earlier in discussion of tragedy *"ta de moi pathemata mathemata gegone,"* which connects knowledge with experience. Strictly speaking, it is *pathemata*—passion—that is connected with *mathemata*—knowledge; if knowledge is, as Kenneth Burke suggests, a state, then the connection is between *status* and *pathos*. The state within which one exists is a passion which one undergoes, and it is the basis upon which action occurs. This is consistent with a Lutheran understanding of faith as passion and of work as the fruit that springs from it.

The work that springs from faith, the action that springs from passion, transforms the world. In acting on the world, human beings transform it. The implication is that confession as *act* transforms *status* and thus itself becomes a new source of *pathemata* or experience. This identifies action as mediator between *status* and *confessionis*.

Confession is both the act of confessing and the product of that action: it is both noun and verb. More importantly, it is both process and product. As product, it becomes not act but result, a state. Unless confession is simply to be taken as identical with *status*, it must remain a dynamic process, a continuous interaction of *status* and *actus*.

To identify "act" as mediator between *status* and *confessionis* is to identify the task of ethics not so much with the question "What ought I to do?" as with the question "What is God doing in the world, and how are we to respond?" (Lehmann, 1976). The point is to emphasize that our action is response, traditionally identified as "vocation." The ongoing act of confessing, springing as it does from the passion of faith, takes the form of vocation: God's call, our response. Certainly since the time of the Protestant Reformation and probably long before, this vocation has been conceived in the broadest possible sense (de Waal, 1984). The act of confessing *is* the vocation of the people of God. To name that act, to tell it, is profession.

Profession, then, like confession, is both act (in the form of response) and product (in the form of story). Also like confession, it becomes, as product, a new source of experience, a transformation of the basis of response. If the connection between profession and confession is a valid one, profession must also be a dynamic relationship of *status* and *actus* if it is to avoid becoming identical with the *status quo*.

2. Profession

Sociological studies of professionalization have identified it as a sequence: establishment of a professional association is followed by a change of name, a code of ethics, and political agitation aimed at support from the public power (Larson, 1966). This is analogous to the process of confession, in which a community emerges, identifies itself as a community by distinguishing itself from other communities, and solidifies as a political entity. This has sometimes been identified as a transition from confessing community to confessional church. The act of confessing itself—and the act of professing—defines a community with identifiable boundaries and a culture that is capable of reproducing and maintaining the community. Both the act of confessing and the act of professing transform *status* into *ethos*, a dwelling place. A code of ethics should not be cut off from its confession or its profession; to confess or to profess is to create an ethic. To codify it in such a way as to separate it from the act of confessing and professing is to render it lifeless and oppressive.

The rise of modern professions roughly coincides with the rise of modern corporate capitalism. The traditional professions of divinity, law, and medicine, with their connection to religion and a social elite, did not depend on public perception or acceptance for their status. Status was primarily a function of the social class of clientele and the class from which practitioners were drawn. This meant that practitioners who served growing middle class and lower class populations were separated from practitioners serving the aristocracy, not on the basis of skill or service provided, but purely on the basis of class association. It also meant that those serving the growing bourgeois population depended not on their association with traditional professions but on public perception of their skill and competence for survival. What had been a traditional association based almost exclusively on inherited class status was gradually transformed into an association based on public perception of skill and competence (Larson, 1966).

Already the religious vocations as professions had provided some means for movement from lower to higher classes on the basis of practice, but this was not so much tied to skillful practice as to profession of a traditional rule. Monastic reform movements seem to have arisen especially at times when profession and practice appeared widely separated (Southern, 1973). These reform movements may well provide the key to understanding the mutual transformation of profession and practice.

For the modern practitioners cut off after the middle ages from traditional professions but associated with the increasingly powerful middle class, public perception became the key factor in determining the success with which they could practice their profession. With the emergence of capitalism, this meant that the professions became associated with the formation of markets. Outside the relatively small sphere of the socially elite, the professions were circumscribed by their ability to create public perception of the importance of their services and their competence to deliver them.

It is significant that the professions produced services and so had to transform their services into commodities to create and compete in markets within emerging capitalism. Professional practice itself became a commodity to be packaged and sold; this meant, in a sense, that the professional *was* the commodity. It led to standardization of practice by standardization of education and imposition of credential requirements. The professional schools emerged as the factories of modern professions. Their products, professionals, depended on public perception of skill and competence which gradually came to be identical to association with a professional school, a professional association, and a professional credential. What began as a popular designation or acknowledgment of competent practice became a popular perception of competent practice derived from association with an elite group. The modern transformation of professions, like earlier transformation of monastic order, tended to drive a wedge between profession and practice.

This transformation reshaped the traditional professions as well. A case in point is medicine, where the professional status of doctors increasingly depended on the insistence not only that they were competent in "arts of healing" but also that others who were not doctors were incompetent. This led to increasing dependence on an elite group for healing; some have argued that this also led to a general deterioration of public health (Illich, 1977). At the same time, practitioners such as midwives, whose status depended not on professional association or certification but on practice and a perception of successful or competent practice, were denied professional status (Rich, 1977). It is a measure of the success of the medical profession in creating markets that this denial of professional status came to be equated in public perception with a denial of competence. Again, it is not clear that childbearing became safer or better with this transformation; but a professional monopoly was achieved.

The connection between practice and profession and the apparent tendency of the process identified as professionalization to drive a wedge between them is of particular importance for ethics. Profession is, as has already been suggested, a public statement analogous to confession; where it becomes separated from practice, we have moved close to a purely traditional code that may ensure social status but not competent or good action.

The experience of midwives suggests that professionalization could lead to certification of practitioners not on the basis of competence but on the basis of professional association. This has particular significance for contemporary efforts to professionalize important activities such as childcare. It is probably more than coincidence that both of these activities have traditionally been dominated by women and that they tend to be accorded low status in spite of their obvious importance. It has been suggested in the case of childcare that one of the problems facing professionalization of the field is the perception that everyone knows how to care for children (Katz and Ward, 1978). There is a curious connection between a skill's popular base or presumed popular accessibility and diminishment of its value or importance. The connection is curious because a popular base or popular accessibility is not necessarily connected with competence. It is also curious because popular base or popular accessibility is not necessarily connected, either directly or inversely, with importance. Even if everyone did know how to care for children (and there is overwhelming evidence that not everyone does), caring for children would still be a vital activity in any society interested in survival. Caring for them well would be vital in any society interested in becoming more fully human.

Current attempts to define early childhood education provide an excellent test case with which to explore the possibility of a popular profession firmly connected with practice and not dependent on elitism. From the perspective of professional ethics, it should suggest a transformation of profession generally toward closer connection with practice and greater awareness of popular roots (but for a radically different perspective, see Schaefer, 1984).

One of the characteristics of modern professions consistently noted by sociologists is creation of public perception that the service rendered by the professional is a need and that the professional is the only one competent to provide it. As has already been suggested, this is associated with transformation of the professional into a commodity and the creation of a market for the commodity (Larson, 1977).

When we focus on childcare as a profession, we discover that the need is present without any effort to create it: children are simply unable to care for themselves and are largely dependent on adults to provide the care necessary for survival. A quick glance at other professions reveals that this is not unique: human beings also have a need for health; and, in times of illness, this appears as an extension of the need for care present in children. That the human condition is one of interdependence may provide the basis for discussing needs of any kind. One problem, it seems, is identifying real needs as opposed to those that are fabricated. Another problem is distinguishing the existence of a need from existence of the professional as the commodity that fills it. This is the same problem identified earlier in speaking of the emergence of modern professions. Does professional status relate to competence in addressing a real need, or does it relate to certification that the professional was produced by the officially recognized process?

The difficulty confronted by childcare workers in securing professional status is, as already suggested, connected with this. Everyone needs care; that the human race has survived to this point attests to the fact that this care has been provided—at least in many cases. This is easily translated into the assumption that appropriate care has been and continues to be readily available. In capitalism, it also translates into the assumption that what is widely available is of little economic value, which is arguably the only type of value recognized in capitalism. Professionalization has typically responded to this by insisting that only those securing a particular certification are qualified to address the need. This restricts the availability of a service and places control of that availability in the hands of the association responsible for certification. This typically renders the service more costly, elevates the status of those providing the service, and restricts the role of those who need the service in determining either its quality or its availability. There is certainly a temptation among those involved in early childhood education to emulate this process, evidenced by the recent movement of early childhood programs into public schools.

The professionalization of other parts of education should serve as a warning here (Silin, 1985). It has led to a steadily diminishing familial role as well as steadily deteriorating quality of education. It has implied that only those certified as members of the profession are capable of teaching. It has virtually eliminated the "clients" (both students and families) from any viable role in controlling the quality or type of services available (Goodman, 1964; Illich, 1970).

One of the most widely praised contemporary transformations of an educational system, the Chicago Public Schools, is illustrative. After a protracted grassroots struggle, a high degree of local control, including representation of parents, local communities, and teachers, was legislated. Local School Councils with substantial decision making power came into being with unprecedented electoral participation. These Councils confronted massive problems resulting from decades of entrenched bureaucratic abuse. They were promptly blamed for the problems and swept aside by mayoral fiat, subsequently given legislative approval. A manager who has neither certification nor professional expertise was given almost total control over day to day operation of the school system, which he has proceeded to run "like a business," to use the vernacular. It is this mayoral coup and the elevation of managerial expertise that have been widely praised in popular accounts, while removal of students, parents, and teachers from decision making has been largely ignored.

The relevant question is whether elimination of "clients" from any viable role in controlling quality or type of services available—and the associated elevation of managerial expertise—is a necessary part of the process of professionalization and whether this has anything to do with the meaning of "profession" in its relation to "ethics." This poses two related problems. One is the transformation of need into neediness that turns communities of persons into clients. The other is the elevation of exchange noted in Chapter Two. As a result of this elevation, managerial skill comes to be valued over practical ability to meet human needs.

The need for childcare is not a recent development, nor is the need for quality childcare. The increasingly apparent difficulty of providing that care exclusively in the home is, in a sense, a recent development. I say "in a sense" because traditional family structures provided for an extensive support network beyond the home in the form of extended families. As those networks have broken down, at least partly under the pressure of capitalist economic development, the need for alternatives has become increasingly intense. To the extent that the desire to professionalize early childhood education responds to that need, it is connecting profession with practice rather than driving a wedge between them. The profession is a statement of a vocation to ensure quality care where it is needed—outside the home. This clearly identifies the professional's primary responsibility as being to the child and his or her family. The vocation emerges in a particular state produced by social-economic transformation. The practice of the profession is in turn directed toward transforming that state. The profession is not creation of a monopoly in childcare insisting that only those certified are capable of providing quality care. It is instead a commitment from those who profess to provide such care. The point is not competition with families, including extended families, but cooperation with them. The point is not to create a market for professionals or for a particular service, but rather to address a need. Because those in need are so vulnerable, it is doubly important to insure that the need is being competently and responsibly addressed (Katz and Ward, 1978).

That is most likely to be accomplished where profession grows out of the practice of vocation, and it is most likely to make sense where there is a community of discourse including those serving as well as those served. It is most likely to emerge where it is recognized that the servers and the served are the same people, all called to respond faithfully; where action becomes response and where responsiveness, not adherence to a rule, is the measure of action.

Chapter Eleven

PRACTICING VALUE

John Sayles's *Lone Star* opens with two characters in a field somewhere in Texas. One is wearing headphones attached to a metal detector, searching for old bullets that, as we learn later, he melts down and turns into objects of art. The other is identifying as many different varieties of cactus as he can find. The character identifying the cactus says "If you're going to live in a place, you need to learn something about it." Shortly thereafter, they uncover a skeleton that becomes a major element in development of the plot. The end of the film is a scene that again includes two characters, one of whom (she is Latina) says to the other, "Forget the Alamo." This is a plot that exposes several key themes for ethics:

- If you are going to live in a place, you need to learn something about it.
- To learn something about a place, you are going to have to dig into it.
- If you start digging in the place where you live, you are going to uncover some skeletons. The bad news in that is that exposing buried skeletons is almost always painful. The good news is that buried skeletons almost always make good stories.
- We live between memory and forgetfulness: to understand what we mean by "we," we have to remember—but to get on with our lives, we also have to forget.

Toni Morrison reminded us in *Beloved* that every step we take in this country is a step into a place of buried skeletons saturated with a thousand intersecting histories of violence. Though we cannot not remember—because the blood of our brothers and sisters cries out from the ground, some stories are not stories to pass on.

1. *Kenosis*

It is serendipitous—a gift of grace—for ethicists reflecting in a "Western" context that the Greek word (*ethos*) from which ethics derives originally designated a dwelling place for animals and that Christianity has been constructed around a story of the birth of God in a stable. In the case of Christianity, the stable has served as a symbol for the condescension or self-emptying (*kenosis*) of God and as a reflection of God's solidarity with the poor. As the locus for the story of the Incarnation, it is a potentially significant answer to a question that is probably as old as humankind: Where do we meet God? Christianity's foundation myth suggests that we meet God with the poor, the outcast, and the homeless on the edge of civilization, where non-human animals are more at home than human ones.

The stable, a dwelling place for animals, is a human construction that is both in and out of the human world of civilization. In the story of Jesus's birth, the stable becomes home for Mary, Joseph, and Jesus only because there is no room for them in the inn. Jesus's birth takes place where animals are at home; but what is home for animals is a temporary shelter on the periphery of a temporary home for human beings who are in the middle of a journey.

Another place where animals dwell is their haunt, a place to which they habitually return. This is not a human construction at all; what makes it home is the act of habitual return.

Robert Frost once described home as "the place where, when you have to go there, they have to take you in."

Ethics is connected with home, but it is also connected with temporary shelter on the edge of the human world in the middle of a human journey. It is connected with custom, habit, habitual return, and—as Frost's image suggests—necessity. And it is connected with a taking in that directs our attention to the edge, where we meet God and other strangers.

To begin, as Christian ethics does, with the question of where we meet God and the intuition that the meeting takes place "on the edge" puts us in the paradoxical position of beginning at the end of the world rather than at the beginning. This is not only paradoxical but also, as Dietrich Bonhoeffer was aware, dangerous. By beginning at the end, we run the risk of absolutizing ends that are not absolute. However, by not beginning at the end, we run the risk of absolutizing the "middles" in which we live and forgetting that they have ends. It is on this basis that Bonhoeffer (1965) asserted that the first task of Christian ethics is to invalidate the knowledge of good and evil, making Christian ethics "a critique of all ethics simply as ethics."

Beginning at the end results in a critique of all ethics simply as ethics for reasons similar to those summarized by Lewis Carroll's Cheshire Cat in conversation with a bewildered (and lost) Alice searching for an answer to one of the most important variations on the "standard" ethical question of action, "Which way ought I to go?":

'That depends a good deal on where you want to get to,' said the Cat.
'I don't much care where—' said Alice.
'Then it doesn't much matter which way you go,' said the Cat.
'—so long as I get *somewhere*,' Alice added as an explanation.

'Oh, you're sure to do that,' said the Cat, 'if you only walk long
enough.'
Alice felt that this could not be denied, so she tried another question.
'What sort of people live around here?'
'In *that* direction,' the Cat said, waving its right paw round, 'lives a
Hatter: and in *that* direction,' waving the other paw, 'lives a March
Hare. Visit either you like: they're both mad.'
'But I don't want to go among mad people,' Alice remarked.
'Oh, you can't help that,' said the Cat: 'we're all mad here. I'm mad.
You're mad.'
'How do you know I'm mad?' said Alice.
'You must be,' said the Cat, 'or you wouldn't have come here' (Carroll,
pp. 88-89).

The Cat begins with an awareness of the importance of where we are and
describes it as a situation which is madness by definition. He moves through the
commonplace that to be is to be somewhere and to the assertion—at Alice's
prompting—that "somewheres," the places where we are, are defined in large
part by the characters that inhabit them. The places where we are are connected
by our action—our movement from one to another—and the places, the action,
and the characters contribute to who we are and where we are going.

In the tradition of confessional theology, particularly as embodied in
Bonhoeffer (1906-1945) and Karl Barth (1886-1968), situations that are so
distorted as to be structurally synonymous with madness have been labeled
"times for confessing" and considered under the rubric of *status confessionis*.
They have given rise to confessions that struggle to deal with the condition
rightly imposed by the Cheshire Cat (which way we ought to go depends a great
deal on where we want to get to) while taking seriously the condition necessarily
imposed by a distorted world (Lutheran World Federation, 1983; Barndt and
Schroeder, 1988). *Status confessionis* is an eschatological image of trial in which
one's present is viewed in terms of one's end; existence is being in the presence
of God, being called to testify of the presence of God in a fallen world. That
vision of a distorted present in terms of an end that is "where we want to get to"
is both ethically and politically transformative.

2. Reading the West

For Bonhoeffer, the vision of a distorted present involved a reading of the history
of "the West" analogous to the Cheshire Cat's reading of the place and time in
which Alice encountered him. His most extended versions of that reading are
"Ethics as Formation," which appears in the posthumously published *Ethics* (and

which Clifford Green has convincingly argued should be read as the beginning of the second of three blocks that make up the book, the one that constitutes the bulk of the text), and a series of letters to Eberhard Bethge written from prison during 1944 (Bonhoeffer, 1972, pp. 324-329; pp. 335-337; pp. 339-342; pp. 343-347; pp. 357-363; pp. 369-370).

"Ethics as Formation" begins with a reflection on the absence of concern for theoretical ethics precipitated by Bonhoeffer's conviction that most people at the time he was writing (around 1940) were too deeply embroiled in the pressing problems posed by practical ethics to concern themselves with the theoretical. Preoccupation with the practical, to the extent that it means giving precedence to the concrete rather than the abstract, is critically important to Bonhoeffer's own approach to ethics. But he is concerned with the extent to which the popular preoccupation was entangled with a "failure of *reasonable* people to perceive either the depths of evil or the depths of the holy" (Bonhoeffer, 1965, p. 65). Writing from the depths of Hitler's Germany, Bonhoeffer himself is preoccupied with the failure of ethics, as understood by "reasonable" people, to sustain resistance. There are obvious reasons for that preoccupation, which became the basis for a "realistic" ethic grounded in a careful reading of history, in the last years of his life.

Bonhoeffer points to the failure of reason, will, conscience, duty, freedom, and private virtue as bases for ethics, then proposes a "Christological" alternative (Bonhoeffer, 1978; Bonhoeffer, 1988; Yerkes, 1978). The only adequate basis for Christian ethics, he insists, is Christ; and this means that it is grounded not in a general or abstract principle but in a particular and concrete encounter with God in humankind. God, Bonhoeffer insists, did not become an abstract principle; God became a human being.

This is an important point of distinction between Bonhoeffer's reading of Hegel and what has come to be known as Hegelianism. For Bonhoeffer, the emphasis is on the human being; for Hegelianism, it is often on the human being as embodiment of an abstract principle, Reason. The Christological alternative is thus also incarnational, and it is this incarnational character of ethics that makes it so important to read history rather than simply being swept along by it. If human history is where we meet God, then it is of central importance from a theological as well as an anthropological perspective.

Bonhoeffer understands the failure of that long list of noble bases for human ethics in the context of the struggle that ensues when "an old world ventures to take up arms against a new one and when a world of the past hazards an attack against the superior forces of the commonplace and mean" (Bonhoeffer, 1965, p. 68). The patron saint of this struggle is Don Quixote, and there is good reason to take a second look at that patron of impossible causes. The second look, as Kirkpatrick Sale has suggested, might lead us to read *Don Quixote* rather than the *Aeneid* as the foundation myth of "Western" culture.

The problem posed by Don Quixote's struggle on behalf of the old world against the new is how to see the world as it is. Bonhoeffer asserts that the wise person is the one "who sees reality as it is, and who sees into the depths of things" (Bonhoeffer, 1965, p. 68). This raises the question of the relative wisdom of Don Quixote and Aeneas. Was Don Quixote wise when he saw dragons and princesses where others saw only windmills and servants? Was he wise when he looked back and saw those visions as delusions? Was Aeneas wise when he looked at the shield of Pallas in Turnus's hand and saw the murder of Pallas? All of these questions suggest that what we see and what we do are inextricably connected.

For Bonhoeffer, to see reality as it is, to see into the depths of things, is to see reality in God. There are hints here both of the Hegelian shape of Bonhoeffer's historical and epistemological outlook and of the limitedness of that shape: though Bonhoeffer is reluctant to follow Hegel in explicitly affirming that without the world, God would not be God, he is more than willing to insist that without God, the world would not be the world. His reluctance to follow the seemingly more radical version of Hegel's assertion stems from a clear-sighted understanding of the dangerous tendency to deify the world; it does not prevent him from later recognizing that the hypothesis of God may have no place in a world come of age. If one is to see God, one must look at the world; and if one is to see Jesus, one must look at humankind. "Jesus," Bonhoeffer writes, "is not *a* man. He is *man*" (Bonhoeffer, 1965, p. 72).

That this is an ethical as much as an epistemological problem becomes progressively clearer over the four or five year span from the composition of this text to the last of the prison letters to Bethge. The problem is not how to be redeemed from the world or to be given a place outside the world from which to move it but how to be redeemed .into it. And that means both how to be empowered to live in it and how to be enabled to recognize it. For Bonhoeffer, "to be conformed with the Incarnate is to have the right to be the man [or woman] one really is" (Bonhoeffer, 1965, p. 81).

Bonhoeffer is inclined to insist that the end is in the beginning (Bonhoeffer, 1997). We live from the end of time because the eschatological event of incarnation, God's taking on of human flesh, has already happened. This means that "the point of departure for Christian ethics is the body of Christ" (Bonhoeffer, 1965, p. 83). And it means, because "the Church is nothing but a section of humanity in which Christ has really taken form," that the point of departure is "the form of Christ in the form of the Church."

The latter form became increasingly problematic for Bonhoeffer in the course of the *Kirchenkampf*, and this problematization of the form of the Church is one of his great strengths. To the extent that the Church is the body of Christ, it is a living being, that, like all living beings, is not only formed but also in formation. The important thing, as Bonhoeffer wrote in one of his letters from

prison, "is that we should be able to discover from the fragment of our life how
the whole was arranged and planned, and what material it consists of"
(Bonhoeffer, 1972, p. 219). Remember the first of Luther's 95 theses: the real
problem is not so much the meaning of "repentance" as the possibility of a
"whole" life. We confront the Church in the world; it is not an Archimedean
point. We confront it both as a crucified, broken body that challenges us to
discern the whole in the parts and as a resurrected body that "takes form among
us here and now" (Bonhoeffer, 1965, pp. 84, 85).

Bonhoeffer reads history because that is where we meet God. He also reads
it with the consciousness that "our" history sets us "objectively in a definite
nexus of experiences, responsibilities and decisions from which we cannot free
ourselves again except by an abstraction. We live, in fact, within this nexus,
whether or not we are in every respect aware of it" (Bonhoeffer, 1965, p. 87).
Bonhoeffer reads history because that is where we—both as individuals and as
communities—become who we are.

Those are not two reasons for reading history, but two ways of speaking
about one reason. In our encounter with history, we encounter God, and it is that
encounter that empowers us to be who we are.

When he later speaks about the penultimate and the ultimate, Bonhoeffer
explains that the penultimate must always precede the ultimate temporally; that
the ultimate is not, however, to be understood as resulting from the penultimate;
and that the penultimate (even though it comes first) is entirely dependent on the
ultimate. Without God the world would not be the world—nor would "we" be
"we." But before we encounter God, we encounter the world in history, and it is
in the encounter that we become—the encounter is the becoming.

Bonhoeffer is closer to Luther and the Hebrew prophets at this point than
was Hegel to the extent that Hegel saw the "abstraction" by which we "free
ourselves" as the "point" of our historical-philosophical inquiry. To the extent
that Hegel saw history as a process within which consciousness becomes
conscious of itself and thereby "transcends" itself, he departed from the profound
"this worldliness" that Luther appropriated from Hebrew Scripture. Bonhoeffer
would be more inclined to describe the process as one of conformation in which
human being comes into being in encounter with the fully human reality
embodied in Christ. This, I think, is what he must have had in mind in the
prison letters when he told Eberhard Bethge that Christianity is not a religion
of redemption. "Redemption myths," he wrote, "arise from human boundary
experiences, but Christ takes hold of a man [or woman] at the center of his [or
her] life" (Bonhoeffer, 1972, pp. 336-337).

That our reading of history is an encounter may identify it as an action or
as a passion. As an action, it is formation: we make history, and we are most
likely to make it in our image. Bonhoeffer, like Kierkegaard, was critical of
Hegel's tendency to see his own time and place as the end point toward which

all previous history had developed and in which all previous history took shape. But, like Kierkegaard, he was also conscious of the fact that to the extent that we become subjects of history we can only see it—and make it—from the places and times in which we stand. We cannot step outside the world, and to claim that we have done so is to deify our place and time while despising humanity in a way that Bonhoeffer, following Luther, identifies as decidedly unchristian. As a passion, it is conformation: we are made by history, and to the extent that God is the subject of history we are made in God's image. Bonhoeffer was acutely conscious of the extent to which the deification of the human as subject of history could result in profound deformation and dehumanization of the human as its object. For evidence, he had only to look at the Total State of Nazism.

Bonhoeffer's consciousness of the profound deformation and dehumanization so prevalent as a product of the historical nexus within which he lived is the backdrop against which he speaks of "the Christian west." For Bonhoeffer, that backdrop is one in which God's action in history is obscured and which therefore poses two practical questions: What is it about the history of the "Christian west" that has obscured God as the subject of history? and What can be done to facilitate encounter with God in the context of this history?

Both questions contribute to a definition of the Church and its work, though the first does this only by defining the larger context within which the Church and its work exist. Bonhoeffer's answer to the first question goes some way toward describing what he sees as the order of the old world that struggles against the new world constituted by the form of Christ in the Church. Bonhoeffer's reading of the old world is shaped in part by that world, as indicated, perhaps, in his choice of the word "inheritance," *Erbe*, which had both biological and historical dimensions in the ideology of National Socialism, and it is predicated on the assumption that the old world renders responsibility difficult to the extent that it places obstacles in the way of encountering and therefore responding to God. The form of the Church, for Bonhoeffer, is that space in the world that enables encounter with and therefore response to God. It is the response to God in the world and therefore in humankind that constitutes responsible action (Bonhoeffer, 1965, pp. 222-254).

Bonhoeffer distinguishes "the west" from the rest of the world by suggesting that we look back to our forbears not as "ancestors who are made the object of worship and veneration" but as "witnesses of the entry of God into history" (Bonhoeffer, 1965, p. 89). This tendency to think of only "the West" as having a history is characteristic of the German historiography with which Bonhoeffer was familiar, both in its Hegelian and Spenglerian forms. It raises questions about the meaning of "myth" and "history" that I will return to later. Jesus, according to Bonhoeffer, is "the continuity of our history." This obviously involves a degree of exclusivity that demands reexamination and repudiation: it is not a story to pass on. But, to Bonhoeffer's credit, it does not lead him to an exclusive focus on Christian Scripture that excludes, devalues, or simply subsumes Hebrew Scripture, a focus that was undeniably tempting to Christian theologians in the Nazi context (Ericksen, 1985). Instead, it leads first to a Christocentric then to a more broadly incarnational interpretation of Hebrew Scripture and to a reminder that "an expulsion of the Jews from the west must necessarily bring with it an expulsion of Christ. For Jesus Christ was a Jew" (Bonhoeffer, 1965, p. 90; Kuske, 1976).

This is important not only as a repudiation of Hitler's attack on the Jewish community of Europe but also because it establishes one source of the "inheritance" of "the west" in Bonhoeffer's reading of history. He looked to Hebrew Scripture and to Judaism as one of the sources out of which this entity called "the west" was born. It is, significantly, the Jewish community to whom we look first as witnesses. And when we look, one of the skeletons we uncover is a long history of Christian anti-Semitism.

Greco-Roman antiquity is a second source in Bonhoeffer's reading that is subsequently transformed into several sources with distinct implications. As he tells the story, the Roman Hellenistic world is important because it is the "time when the time of God was fulfilled" and because it is "the world which God took to Himself in the incarnation" (Bonhoeffer, 1965, p. 90). This suggests that God became incarnate not just in a particular person but also in the world within which that person lived. That the second part of this suggestion would follow from the first may seem obvious, but it has important implications: when God became human, God took on the whole world. This parallels the theme repeated several times in *Ethics* of Jesus as *man* [sic] rather than *a* man. It also amounts to a reaffirmation of the characteristically Hegelian and characteristically Lutheran connection between God and the world.

Though Bonhoeffer gives special significance to the Greco-Roman heritage of "the west," he splits it by identifying the Roman heritage as coming to represent "the combination and assimilation of antiquity with the Christian element" and the Greek heritage as coming to represent "opposition and hostility to Christ" (Bonhoeffer, 1965, p. 90). Given the role of the Roman government in the crucifixion, this may seem a bit odd, but Bonhoeffer appears to have in mind the identification of the Church with Rome that gradually occurred over the first several centuries of Christianity. And he appears to have in mind the tendency of "Western" thinkers who wanted an alternative to Christianity to look to the Greeks and their mythology as a pre-Christian and often anti-Christian option. This had particular importance in his context because of Nietzsche's appropriation of Greek philosophy and its employment by some architects of Nazi ideology.

Bonhoeffer traces this approach to the Greek tradition back to the German Reformation. The Roman tradition had been passed on to Europe in general and Germany in particular in a more or less unbroken line. In fact, Bonhoeffer points out with some justification that the histories of Europe began in the encounter with Rome and that, as Rome became inextricably identified with Christianity in the West, those histories began in the encounter with Christ transmitted through the medium of Rome. Western Europe saw itself as the inheritor of Roman antiquity and therefore appropriated Roman Christianity and Roman foundation myths, including the *Aeneid*, reinterpreted through Christian eyes. Luther's turn away from Rome meant a turn toward Greece because there were only two "Western" alternatives—though one might ask why the alternative had to be "Western" and what "Western" could possibly mean in this context.

In Bonhoeffer's reading, there is one inheritance with four sources, three of which are joined together in the historical figure of Jesus and one of which is viewed as "pre-Christian":

- first is the Jewish tradition, particularly the tradition of the Hebrew prophets;
- second is the Greek tradition, particularly the tradition of Greek philosophy and tragic drama interpreted as "humanistic";
- third is the Hellenistic tradition, which is a melding of Greek and Roman tradition and which is the world into which Jesus was born;
- fourth is the Roman tradition, which is the tradition of Roman Christianity.

Bonhoeffer could argue that the person of Jesus ties all these sources together to the extent that the Greek tradition is appropriated through the Hellenistic world. But he is interested in the "consciously anti-Christian" (not just anti-Roman) conjuring up of the Greek heritage that he sees as characteristic of Germany's attitude toward antiquity.

The Reformation shattered "the *corpus christianum*, the historical order of the Christian west, which was ruled and held together by Emperor and Pope in the name of Jesus Christ" (Bonhoeffer, 1965, p. 94). Bonhoeffer attributes this to Luther's conviction that the unity of the faith could not reside in any political power, which gave rise to the Lutheran understanding of "two kingdoms." He insists that, while Luther did not lose sight of the fact that God is the sovereign of both kingdoms, many Lutherans and others misunderstood the two kingdoms as implying "the emancipation and sanctification of the world and of the natural" (Bonhoeffer, 1965, p. 96). Bonhoeffer sees the Lutheran Reformation as providing the background against which a proper distinction of two spheres of God's activity in the world could be transformed into a vision of the world as consisting of one sphere in which God is sovereign and one sphere in which God is not. This split becomes an important theme for his ethical analysis and has been an important tool with which to explain the "Lutheran" and more broadly

Protestant tradition of withdrawal into quietism and personal piety that played so disastrously into Hitler's hands in Germany.

The misunderstanding of "two kingdoms" as an "emancipation and sanctification of the world and of the natural" is seen as the basis for emergence of western technology as mastery rather than service. To the extent that "the natural" becomes independent of God, there is a renewed western emphasis on dominating it, as though the issue of sovereignty is in doubt and must be established primarily through technological means. Bonhoeffer does not reject western technology and is in fact critical of those who do. He asserts that "the age of technology is a genuine heritage of our western history. We must come to grips with it. We cannot return to the pretechnical era" (Bonhoeffer, 1965, p. 99). This poses the obvious problem of how, precisely, to come to grips with it, a problem that still plagues us.

For Bonhoeffer, then, the Lutheran Reformation is the starting point of an independent secular sphere from which God is excluded and a religious sphere to which the Church is increasingly confined. It is also the moment of birth of a western technological tradition of dominance over nature in the name of humankind as opposed to service to humankind through nature in the name of God. This is not to say that Bonhoeffer believed Luther intended these consequences; he expressly denied this in a Reformation Day letter to his parents written in 1943 (Bonhoeffer, 1972, p. 123). But he became increasingly conscious of the power of unintended consequences and secondary motivations during his time in prison.

Bonhoeffer cites the French Revolution as the moment of birth of modern nationalism (Bonhoeffer, 1965, p. 100). He distinguishes the "nation" (which is organic) from the "state" (which is institutional) and identifies France with the former, Prussia with the latter. "Prussia," Bonhoeffer asserts, wished to be neither nationalistic nor international. In this respect its thought was more western than was that of the Revolution" (Bonhoeffer, 1965, pp. 100-101). In the defeat of Prussia by France, Bonhoeffer sees the triumph of technology, mass movements, and nationalism which became the inheritance bequeathed by the Revolution to the western world. His reading suggests that the Reformation opened the way to a misunderstanding that was then transformed by the French Revolution into this deadly inheritance. That it is deadly in Bonhoeffer's eyes results in part from the bitter conflict it contains: "The masses and nationalism," he writes, "are hostile to reason. Technology and the masses are hostile to nationalism. Nationalism and technology are hostile to the masses" (Bonhoeffer, 1965, p. 102).

It is no more surprising that Bonhoeffer, a German Lutheran pastor, would read the French Revolution through the lens of the German Reformation than that Burke, a British MP, read it earlier through the lens of England's "Glorious Revolution." "Luther's great discovery of the freedom of the Christian man," he writes, "and the Catholic heresy of the essential good in man combined to produce the deification of man. But, rightly understood, the deification of man is the proclamation of nihilism" (Bonhoeffer, 1965, p. 103). That nihilism is embodied for Bonhoeffer in Nazi Germany.

In his *Ethics*, it is clear that Bonhoeffer sees the Christian Church as the guardian of the western inheritance against the nihilism embodied in Nazism. The "Western inheritance" he has in mind is the form of Christ, the dwelling of God with humankind that is communicated by both Hebrew and Christian Scripture and which "the west" first encountered in the Roman Church. The "decay" of the west derives from its refusal "to accept its historical inheritance for what it is" (Bonhoeffer, 1965, p. 108). That this vision continues in the prison correspondence is evidenced by the fact that the "worldly Christianity" Bonhoeffer was struggling to articulate there was directed toward enabling humankind to encounter God in the world, even when the hypothesis of God had been discarded. This reading suggests an interpretation of the *theologia crucis* which would insist that we encounter God in the death of God and provides an important background against which to read subsequent "death of God" theology.

3. Embracing the World

Bonhoeffer's reading of history is Hegelian, but it is also radically Christocentric, incarnational, and concrete. These characteristics, I believe, gave it a critical edge that the later Hegel and many of his followers lost in their absolutization of the System and their virtual sanctification of the existing state of affairs (Marcuse, 1960). Bonhoeffer's critical edge, the ground under his feet that sustained and supported his resistance, consisted in his willingness to embrace the world rather than attempting to overcome or transcend it.

Bonhoeffer is Hegelian to the extent that both he and Hegel are philosophically and theologically Lutheran: they interpret the world and the Church, which is a subset of the world, Christocentrically by way of a *theologia crucis* in which the absolute negation of God's self-identification with humankind is central. At the heart of Bonhoeffer's appropriation of Hegel and Hegel's appropriation of Luther is God's death on the cross. That death, understood as *kenosis*, is the center of the Church and of the world. God's kenotic act, the death of God on the cross, is the source of the world's being; and it is the foundation of the Church, which, as Bonhoeffer argued early in his theological career, is the unity of act and being. In a distinctly Lutheran fashion, both Hegel and Bonhoeffer assert that God alone acts, or, more accurately, that God alone is a single action: what is commonly understood as human action, whether faith or sin, is passion. The being of human beings is toward God (faith) or toward self (sin)—but, in either case, God is subject (the one who acts) while human beings are objects (the ones acted upon).

But a distinctly Lutheran qualification is attached to this assertion in both Hegel and Bonhoeffer, a qualification that was most famously articulated between Hegel and Bonhoeffer by Søren Kierkegaard: God's action is a passion, and it is the structure of human passion that makes it possible for human beings to become subjects. Kierkegaard criticized Hegel for forgetting that human beings (including Hegel himself!) exist; Bonhoeffer appropriated this criticism, and both suggest that the most un-Lutheran thing about Hegel is his inclination toward Absolute System.

That, too, requires qualification. To the extent that Luther placed the cross at the center of his theology, he was anti-systematic, and his thought was radically open. His later thought, however, and the thought of many of his followers, particularly in the various incarnations of Lutheran orthodoxy, tended toward the closure of System. Bonhoeffer rightly pointed out that reason itself tends toward closure, so that all thought, to the extent that it is scientific and philosophical (that is, rational), is an exercise in system building. It is not, therefore, surprising that Hegel (and, through him, Luther) spawned apparently contradictory philosophical approaches to the world.

There is a radical Hegel and a radically conservative one, just as there are radical and radically conservative Luthers. This, I think, is a crucial point in understanding Bonhoeffer's work (which is not just his writing but his living): the radical and the radically conservative Hegel (or Luther or Bonhoeffer) are not two persons, but one. Dialectical thinkers and dialectical philosophies (and this includes Bonhoeffer and his work) routinely embody contradictions. Luther's thought is revolutionary to the extent that it is a theology of the cross, the negation of every affirmation: as long as the cross is at the center, the system building tendency of reason is held in check, and system building does not degenerate into System. Hegel's thought is revolutionary to the extent that it is a philosophy of absolute negation: as long as absolute negation is at the center, systematization remains open, and we are not banished to the gatehouse. Kierkegaard and Bonhoeffer, as interpreters of Hegel and of Luther, repeatedly remind us of the center: they do not allow us to forget that we exist.

To call Bonhoeffer's work "dialectical" raises the question of his relationship to Barth. Given the close personal and intellectual association between the two, some Bonhoeffer interpreters have tended to read him through Barth, almost as though Barth, who, unlike Bonhoeffer, survived the war and therefore continued developing his thought for some time afterward, completes Bonhoeffer. This is a mistake, both because it devalues Bonhoeffer's contribution and because it overvalues completion. Regardless of one's attitude toward Barth, the overvaluation of completion in interpretation of Bonhoeffer leads to devaluation of the anti-systematic aspects of his thought. Whether one is reading

Kierkegaard or Bonhoeffer, if one sees System as strength, one is likely to discover nothing but weakness.

That may be appropriate in understanding Hegel's contribution through Bonhoeffer to formation of communities of resistance. If one discovers nothing but weakness, one may well have discovered the kenotic center that is constitutive of resistance and community. This insight has been shared by artists, mystics, and poets who have found Nothing in gifts and words that (in Emily Dickinson's image) are "homely" and "hindered," who have continued to seek among those words and gifts because Nothing has a rarely recognized world-renewing power.

This requires one more word about Barth and Barthian interpretations of *kenosis*, which is usually understood as "self-emptying." Reformed theology, including Barthian neo-orthodoxy, has been inclined, I think, to place the emphasis in its understanding of *kenosis* on "self," to the extent that it is interpreted as an act willed or chosen by God: at the center, then, is God's will.

It would certainly be possible to read Kierkegaard or Bonhoeffer in this way as well. In *Fear and Trembling*, for example, Kierkegaard outlines an "anti-ethic" of sorts that depends on the immediate (or transparent) relationship of Abraham with God: either there is a teleological suspension of the ethical, or Abraham is a murderer. The teleological suspension of the ethical assumes that a (human) act is good because God commands it. The salient feature is God's will, and that is the center around which the whole world takes shape.

Bonhoeffer is critical of this reading, however, for two reasons, both of which are important here. First, the reading is radically individualistic, and Bonhoeffer (following Hegel) insists that God is present in community. Where there is no community, there is no God. As Kierkegaard was aware, this renders Abraham's silence problematic and defies any attempt to incorporate the story into a System. God's will is not the salient feature, but Abraham's silence. Which leads to the second criticism: a Lutheran understanding of *kenosis* emphasizes not self, but emptiness. It is not God's will that matters, but God's death.

Karl Marx, another Lutheran interpreter of Hegel, developed this with great clarity in the section of his *Economic and Philosophic Manuscripts of 1844* entitled "Critique of the Hegelian Dialectic and Philosophy as a Whole." There he described absolute negation not as an act of will but as a process of recognition:

> abstraction comprehending itself as abstraction knows itself to be nothing: it must abandon itself—abandon abstraction—and so it arrives at an entity which is its exact opposite—at *nature*. Thus, the entire *Logic* is the demonstration that abstract thought is nothing in itself; that the Absolute Idea is nothing for itself; that only *Nature* is something.

For Marx, this means that "the *mystical* feeling which drives the philosopher forward from abstract thinking to intuiting is *boredom*—the longing for a content." While Marx's critique was developed primarily in response to the *Logic* and Bonhoeffer's 1933 Hegel seminar was a close reading of the *Philosophy of Religion*, both would agree at this point in the assessment of religion as "applied logic." The feeling that drives the philosopher forward may be described as boredom, but it is also a longing for content, for the concrete, the same longing that undergirds religion.

Whether the emphasis in *kenosis* is on self or on emptiness has far-reaching consequences for the understanding and constitution of community, including communities of resistance. Emphasis on self tends toward community constituted by will, while emphasis on emptiness tends toward community constituted by abandonment. The former implies strength, the latter weakness. The former implies a crisis to be resolved by choice, the latter a chronic condition—a condition of need and incompletion.

The distinction, I think, drove much of Bonhoeffer's witness, both in his life and in his writings. The chronic condition grounded in abandonment reveals God's human weakness at the center of the human world. It suggests that human beings form communities, not because we choose to but because we have to. No act of will can "complete" any human being, meaning that there is never a resolution, never a System, in reality. The abandonment communicated by the cross at the center of the world makes all resolutions and all Systems equally false. This means that resistance is not a freely chosen act, incidental to being human, but a human necessity.

It also means, as Hegel, Kierkegaard, and Bonhoeffer were all aware, that we cannot get to the beginning any more than we can get to the end, precisely because we are always in the middle. Bonhoeffer's argument, in his Biblical interpretation as well as in his ethics, made this "being in the middle" even more radical than the one articulated at about the same time by Heidegger. It is not just that we are in the middle, with no *Sein* other than *Dasein*. It is that we are always equally in the middle of the beginning and in the middle of the end.

That we are not only in the middle but also in the middle of the beginning and in the middle of the end means that every act in which we engage is simultaneously beginning, middle, and end. Hence the significance of everydayness in Bonhoeffer (and, earlier, in Kierkegaard). God's absolute absence in identification with humankind transforms time: it directs our attention away from the extraordinary (a theology of glory) toward the ordinary (a theology of the cross). It makes us fundamentally suspicious of heroes (and, by extension, saints).

It is action in the middle of time, in the ordinary, that matters: if you are going to live, you are going to live in a place—and if you are going to live in a place, you need to know something about it. If in getting to know something about it you turn a few bullets into objects of art or beat a few swords into plowshares, so much the better: that is a story we might want to pass on.

REFERENCES

Aristotle. *Works*. Translated under the Editorship of W.D. Ross. London: Oxford University Press, 1963-1968.

Barndt, Joseph and Steven Schroeder. "Confessing Christ and Resisting Capitalism: Is the Prevailing Economic Order a *Status Confessionis?*" In *Economics: A Matter of Faith*. World Council of Churches, Commission on the Churches' Participation in Development, CCPD Documents: Justice and Development, No.11, July 1988.

Barrett Browning, Elizabeth. *Aurora Leigh*. New York: W.W. Norton, 1996. [Based on the fourth edition, published in 1859. First edition published in 1856.]

Berry, Wendell. *The Work of Local Culture*. Iowa City, Iowa: Iowa Humanities Board, 1988.

Biology and the History of the Future: An IUBD/UNESCO Symposium with John Cage, Carl-Goeran Heden, Margaret Mead, John Papaioannou, John Platt, Ruth Sager, and Gunther Stent, presented by C.H. Waddington. Edinburgh: Edinburgh University Press, 1972.

Bonhoeffer, Dietrich. *Ethics*. Translated by Neville Horton Smith. New York: Macmillan, 1965. [Originally published in German in 1949.]

_____. *Letters and Papers from Prison*. Translated by Reginald Fuller, Frank Clarke, John Bowden, *et al*. Edited by Eberhard Bethge. New York: Macmillan, 1972. [Includes material written between 1943 and 1945. Originally published in German in 1970.]

_____. *Christ the Center*, Revised Translation by Edwin H. Robertson. New York: Harper & Row, 1978. [Based on lectures given at the University of Berlin in 1933, reconstructed from student notes by Eberhard Bethge.]

_____. *Dietrich Bonhoeffers Hegel-Seminar 1933*, Nach den Aufzeichnungen von Ferenc Lehel, Herausgegeben von Ilse Tödt. München: Chr. Kaiser Verlag, 1988. [Based on lectures given at the University of Berlin in 1933.]

_____. *Creation and Fall: A Theological Exposition of Genesis 1-3*. Translated by Douglas Stephen Bax. *Dietrich Bonhoeffer Works*, Volume 3.

Minneapolis: Fortress Press, 1997. [Based on lectures given at the University of Berlin in 1932-1933. Originally published in German in 1937.]

Bruner, Jerome. *Actual Minds, Possible Worlds*. Cambridge, Mass.: Harvard University Press, 1986.

Bruns, Gerald. "Poethics: John Cage and Stanley Cavell at the Crossroads of Ethical Theory." In *John Cage: Composed in America*. Edited by Marjorie Perloff and Charles Junkerman. Chicago: University of Chicago Press, 1994.

Buchanan, Scott (Ed.). *The Portable Plato*. Harmondsworth, Eng.: Penguin, 1977.

Burke, Edmund. *Reflections on the Revolution in France*. New York: Penguin, 1986. [Originally published in 1790.]

Burke, Kenneth. *A Grammar of Motives*. Berkeley: University of California Press, 1974. [Originally published in 1945.]

Butler, Octavia. *Dawn*. Xenogenesis Trilogy, Volume One. New York: Warner, 1987.

_____. *Adulthood Rites*. Xenogenesis Trilogy, Volume Two. New York: Warner, 1988.

_____. *Imago*. Xenogenesis Trilogy, Volume Three. New York: Warner, 1989.

Carroll, Lewis. *The Annotated Alice*. New York: Bramhall House, 1960. [*Alice's Adventures in Wonderland* was originally published in 1865, *Through the Looking Glass* in 1872.]

Cervantes, Miguel de. *Don Quixote*. Translated by J.M. Cohen. Baltimore: Penguin, 1972. [First part originally published in Spanish in 1604, second part in 1614.]

Complete Greek Tragedies. Edited by David Grene and Richmond Lattimore. Chicago: University of Chicago Press, 1992.

Crane, Gregory R. (Ed.) *The Perseus Project*. Tufts University. 17 March 2000 <http://www.perseus.tufts.edu>.

Csikszentmihalyi, Mihaly and Eugene Rochberg-Halton. *The Meaning of Things: Domestic Symbols and the Self.* Cambridge, England: Cambridge University Press, 1981.

de Waal, Esther. *Seeking God: The Way of St. Benedict.* Collegeville, Minn.: The Liturgical Press, 1984

Dickinson, Emily. *The Complete Poems of Emily Dickinson.* Edited by Thomas H. Johnson. Boston: Little, Brown and Company, 1961.

Diels, H. *Die Fragmente der Vorsokratiker.* 5th-7th editions. Berlin, 1934-1954.

Douglas, Mary. *Purity and Danger: An Analysis of Concepts of Pollution and Taboo.* 2nd Edition. London: Routledge & Kegan Paul, 1969. [First Edition, 1966.]

_____. *How Institutions Think.* Syracuse, N.Y.: Syracuse University Press, 1986

Ericksen, Robert P. *Theologians Under Hitler: Gerhard Kittel, Paul Althaus, and Emanuel Hirsch.* New Haven, Conn.: Yale University Press, 1985.

Fish, Stanley. *Self-Consuming Artifacts.* Berkeley: University of California Press, 1972.

Fletcher, Richard. *The Barbarian Conversion.* New York: Henry Holt, 1997.

Freeman, Kathleen. *Ancilla to the Pre-Socratic Philosophers.* Cambridge, Mass.: Harvard University Press, 1957.

Furth, Hans G. *Knowledge as Desire: An Essay on Freud and Piaget.* New York: Columbia University Press, 1987.

Gaskell, Elizabeth. *North and South.* New York: Penguin, 1970. [Originally published in 1854-1855.]

Geertz, Clifford. *The Interpretation of Cultures.* New York: Basic Books, 1973.

Gibson, J.J. *The Senses Considered as Perceptual Systems.* Boston: Houghton Mifflin, 1966.

112   REFERENCES

_____. *The Ecological Approach to Visual Perception*. Boston: Houghton Mifflin, 1979.

Gilligan, Carol. *In a Different Voice*. Cambridge, Mass.: Harvard University Press, 1982.

Goodman, Paul. *Compulsory Miseducation and the Community of Scholars*. New York: Vintage, 1964.

Green, Clifford. "The Text of Bonhoeffer's Ethics." In *New Studies in Bonhoeffer's Ethics*. Ed. William J. Peck. Lewiston, New York: Edwin Mellen Press, 1987.

Haraway, Donna. "A Cyborg Manifesto." In *Simians, Cyborgs, and Women: The Reinvention of Nature*. New York: Routledge, 1991.

Hartshorne, Charles. *Creative Synthesis & Philosophic Method*. LaSalle, Ill.: Open Court, 1970.

Hendrix, Jimi. The Jimi Hendrix Experience, *Are You Experienced* (Reprise Records, 6261-2, 1967).

Herman, Edward S. and Noam Chomsky. *Manufacturing Consent: The Political Economy of the Mass Media*. New York: Pantheon Books, 1988.

Hutchinson, D.S. *The Virtues of Aristotle*. London: Routledge & Kegan Paul, 1986.

Illich, Ivan. *Medical Nemesis*. New York: Bantam, 1977.

_____. *Deschooling Society*. New York: Harper and Row, 1970.

Jefferson, Thomas. *Notes on the State of Virginia*. In *The Portable Thomas Jefferson*. Ed. Merrill D. Peterson. New York: Penguin, 1977. [Originally published in 1781-1782.]

Kant, Immanuel. *Foundation of the Metaphysics of Morals*, Translated by Lewis White Beck. Indianapolis: Bobbs-Merrill, 1959. [Originally published in German in 1785.]

Katz, Lilian G. and Evangeline H. Ward. *Ethical Behavior in Early Childhood Education*. Washington, D.C.: National Association for the Education of Young Children, 1978.

Kierkegaard, Søren. *Fear and Trembling*. Translated by Walter Lowrie. Princeton, N.J.: Princeton University Press, 1968. [Originally published in Danish in 1843.]

Kirk, G.S. and J.E. Raven. *The Presocratic Philosophers*. Cambridge, England: Cambridge University Press, 1971. [Originally published in 1957.]

Kohlberg, Lawrence. *Development of Modes of Moral Thinking and Choice in the Years 10 to 16: Kohlberg's Original Study of Moral Development*. Ed. Bill Puka. New York: Garland, 1994. [Reprint of 1958 University of Chicago dissertation.]

Kuske, Martin. *The Old Testament as the Book of Christ: An Appraisal of Bonhoeffer's Interpretation*. Translated by S.T. Kimbrough, Jr. Philadelphia: Westminster, 1976.

Lakoff, George. *Women, Fire, and Dangerous Things: What Categories Reveal About the Mind*. Chicago: University of Chicago Press, 1987.

Larson, Magali Sarfatti. *The Rise of Professionalism: A Sociological Analysis*. Berkeley: University of California Press, 1977.

Lehmann, Paul. *Ethics in a Christian.Context*. New York: Harper & Row, 1976.

Lévinas, Emmanuel. *Nine Talmudic Readings*. Translated by Annette Aronowicz. Bloomington, Indiana: Indiana University Press, 1990. [Originally published in French in 1968.]

Lloyd, Genevieve. *The Man of Reason*. 2nd Edition. Minneapolis, Minn.: University of Minnesota Press, 1993. [First Edition, 1984.]

Locke, John. *An Essay Concerning Human Understanding*. Oxford, England: Clarendon Press, 1975. [First Edition originally published in 1690; Second Edition, 1694.]

Lutheran World Federation. *The Debate on* Status Confessionis*: Studies in Christian Political Theology*. Geneva: Lutheran World Federation, 1983.

MacIntyre, Alasdair. *After Virtue*. Notre Dame, Ind.: University of Notre Dame Press, 1984.

Marcuse, Herbert. *Reason and Revolution*. Boston: Beacon, 1960.

Marx, Karl. *The Economic and Philosophic Manuscripts of 1844*. Translated by Martin Milligan. New York: International Publishers, 1964.

_____. *Capital*. 3 vols. Translated by Samuel Moore and Edward Aveling. New York: International Publishers, 1967. [First edition of Volume 1 originally published in German in 1867. Volume 2 originally published in German in 1885, Volume 3 in 1894.]

Merchant, Carolyn. *The Death of Nature: Women, Ecology, and the Scientific Revolution*. New York: Harper, 1990. [Originally published in 1980.]

Mill, John Stuart. *Utilitarianism*. Indianapolis: Hackett, 1979. [Originally published in 1863.]

Morrison, Toni. *Beloved*. New York: Alfred A. Knopf, 1987.

Mudimbe, V.Y. "The Power of the Greek Paradigm," *South Atlantic Quarterly*, 92:2 (Spring 1993). pp. 361-385.

Nadel, Alan. *Containment Culture: American Narratives, Postmodernism, and the Atomic Age*. Durham, N.C.: Duke University Press, 1996.

Nussbaum, Martha C. *The Fragility of Goodness: Luck and Ethics in Greek Tragedy and Philosophy*. Cambridge, England: Cambridge University Press, 1986.

Paine, Thomas. *The Complete Writings of Thomas Paine*. Ed. Philip S. Foner. New York: Citadel Press, 1969.

Piaget, Jean. *Play, Dreams, and Imitation in Childhood*. Translated by C. Gattegno and F. M. Hodgson. New York: W. W. Norton, 1962. [Originally published in French in 1945.]

_____. *The Moral Judgement of the Child*. Translated by Marjorie Gabain. New York: Free Press, 1965. [Originally published in French in 1932.]

_____. *Six Psychological Studies*. New York: Vintage, 1968. [Originally published in French in 1964.]

_____. *Biology and Knowledge: An Essay on the Relations Between Organic Regulations and Cognitive Processes*. Chicago: University of Chicago Press, 1971. [Originally published in French in 1967].

_____. *Adaptation and Intelligence: Organic Selection and Phenocopy*. Chicago: University of Chicago Press, 1980. [Originally published in French in 1974.]

_____. *The Equilibration of Cognitive Structures*. Chicago: University of Chicago Press, 1985. [Originally published in French in 1975.]

Pieper, Josef. *The Four Cardinal Virtues*. Notre Dame, Ind.: University of Notre Dame Press, 1966. [Pieper's essay on prudence was originally published in German in 1959.]

Plato. *The Dialogues of Plato*. 4th Edition. Translated by B. Jowett. Oxford, England: Clarendon Press, 1969.

Price, Richard. *A Discourse on the Love of Our Country*. New York: Woodstock Books, 1992. [Originally published in 1789.]

Reed, Edward S. *The Necessity of Experience*. New Haven, Conn.: Yale University Press, 1996.

Reineke, Martha J. *Sacrificed Lives: Kristeva on Women and Violence*. Bloomington, Indiana: Indiana University Press, 1997.

Rich, Adrienne. *Of Woman Born*. New York: Bantam, 1977.

Rushdie, Salman. *Midnight's Children*. New York: Alfred A. Knopf, 1981.

Ryle, Gilbert. *Collected Papers*. New York: Barnes & Noble, 1971.

Sale, Kirkpatrick. *The Conquest of Paradise*. New York: Alfred A. Knopf, 1990.

Schaefer, Thomas E. "Professionalism: Foundation for Business Ethics," *Journal of Business Ethics*, 3 (1984), pp. 269-277.

Schroeder, Steven. *The Metaphysics of Cooperation: A Study of F.D. Maurice.* Amsterdam: Rodopi, 1999.

Searle, John. *Minds, Brains, and Science.* Cambridge, Mass.: Harvard University Press, 1984.

Shane, Alex M. *The Life and Works of Evgenij Zamjatin.* Berkeley: University of California Press, 1968.

Silin, Jonathan G. "Authority as Knowledge: A Problem of Professionalization," *Young Children*, 40:3 (1985), pp. 41-46.

Simon, Yves R. *The Definition of Moral Virtue.* New York: Fordham University Press, 1986. [Based on lectures delivered at the University of Chicago in 1957.]

Smith, Adam. *An Inquiry into the Nature and Causes of the Wealth of Nations.* New York: Oxford University Press, 1976. [Originally published in 1776.]

Southern, R.W. *Western Society and the Church in the Middle Ages.* Baltimore: Penguin, 1973.

Spears, Monroe Kirklyndorf. *The Poetry of W.H. Auden: The Disenchanted Island.* New York: Oxford University Press, 1963

Stevens, Wallace. *The Palm at the End of the Mind.* New York: Vintage Books, 1972.

Trible, Phyllis. *Texts of Terror: Literary-feminist Readings of Biblical Narratives.* Philadelphia: Fortress Press, 1984.

Turner, Terence, "Piaget's Structuralism," *American Anthropologist*, 75:2 (1973), pp. 351-373.

Virgil. *The Aeneid of Virgil.* Translated by Allen Mandelbaum. New York: Bantam, 1971.

Vygotsky, Lev. *Thought and Language.* Translated by Alex Kozulin. Cambridge, Mass.: MIT Press, 1986.

Wagner, Roy. *The Invention of Culture.* Revised and Expanded Edition. Chicago: University of Chicago Press, 1981. [Originally published in 1975.]

Walker, David. *David Walker's Appeal, in Four Articles, Together with a Preamble to the Coloured Citizens of the World, but in Particular, and Very Expressly to Those of the United States of America*. New York: Hill and Wang, 1995. [Originally published in 1829.]

Wollstonecraft, Mary. *A Vindication of the Rights of Woman*. New York: Penguin, 1983. [Originally published in 1792.]

Yerkes, James. *The Christology of Hegel*. Missoula, Mont.: Scholars Press, 1978.

Zamyatin, Yevgeney. "On Literature, Revolution, Entropy, and Other Matters." Translated by Mirra Ginsberg. In *A Soviet Heretic*. London: Quartet, 1991. [Originally published in Russian in 1923.]

_____. *We*. Translated by Clarence Brown. New York: Penguin, 1993. [Written in Russian in 1920-1921. First published in English in 1924.]

ABOUT THE AUTHOR

Steven Schroeder lives and writes in Chicago, Illinois. He is the author of three previous books, including *The Metaphysics of Cooperation: A Study of F.D. Maurice*, Volume 84 in the Value Inquiry Book Series.

INDEX

VIBS

The **Value Inquiry Book Series** is co-sponsored by:

American Maritain Association
American Society for Value Inquiry
Association for Process Philosophy of Education
Center for Bioethics, University of Turku
Center for International Partnerships, Rochester Institute of Technology
Center for Professional and Applied Ethics, University of North Carolina at
Charlotte
Centre for Applied Ethics, Hong Kong Baptist University
Centre for Cultural Research, Aarhus University
College of Education and Allied Professions, Bowling Green State University
Concerned Philosophers for Peace
Conference of Philosophical Societies
Global Association for the Study of Persons
Institute of Philosophy of the High Council of Scientific Research, Spain
International Academy of Philosophy of the Principality of Liechtenstein
International Society for Universal Dialogue
Natural Law Society
Philosophical Society of Finland
Philosophy Born of Struggle Association
Philosophy Seminar, University of Mainz
R.S. Hartman Institute for Formal and Applied Axiology
Russian Philosophical Society
Society for Iberian and Latin-American Thought
Society for the Philosophic Study of Genocide and the Holocaust
Society for the Philosophy of Sex and Love
Yves R. Simon Institute.

Titles Published

1. Noel Balzer, *The Human Being as a Logical Thinker.*

2. Archie J. Bahm, *Axiology: The Science of Values.*

3. H. P. P. (Hennie) Lötter, *Justice for an Unjust Society.*

4. H. G. Callaway, *Context for Meaning and Analysis: A Critical Study in the Philosophy of Language.*

5. Benjamin S. Llamzon, *A Humane Case for Moral Intuition.*

6. James R. Watson, *Between Auschwitz and Tradition: Postmodern Reflections on the Task of Thinking.* A volume in **Holocaust and Genocide Studies.**

7. Robert S. Hartman, *Freedom to Live: The Robert Hartman Story, edited by Arthur R. Ellis.* A volume in **Hartman Institute Axiology Studies.**

8. Archie J. Bahm, *Ethics: The Science of Oughtness.*

9. George David Miller, *An Idiosyncratic Ethics; Or, the Lauramachean Ethics.*

10. Joseph P. DeMarco, *A Coherence Theory in Ethics.*

11. Frank G. Forrest, *Valuemetrics*^{N}*: The Science of Personal and Professional Ethics.* A volume in **Hartman Institute Axiology Studies.**

12. William Gerber, *The Meaning of Life: Insights of the World's Great Thinkers.*

13. Richard T. Hull, Editor, *A Quarter Century of Value Inquiry: Presidential Addresses of the American Society for Value Inquiry.* A volume in **Histories and Addresses of Philosophical Societies.**

14. William Gerber, *Nuggets of Wisdom from Great Jewish Thinkers: From Biblical Times to the Present.*

15. Sidney Axinn, *The Logic of Hope: Extensions of Kant's View of Religion.*

16. Messay Kebede, *Meaning and Development.*

17. Amihud Gilead, *The Platonic Odyssey: A Philosophical-Literary Inquiry into the Phaedo.*

34. George David Miller and Conrad P. Pritscher, *On Education and Values: In Praise of Pariahs and Nomads*. A volume in **Philosophy of Education.**

35. Paul S. Penner, *Altruistic Behavior: An Inquiry into Motivation.*

36. Corbin Fowler, *Morality for Moderns.*

37. Giambattista Vico, *The Art of Rhetoric (Institutiones Oratoriae*, 1711-1741), from the definitive Latin text and notes, Italian commentary and introduction by Giuliano Crifo, translated and edited by Giorgio A. Pinton and Arthur W. Shippee. A volume in **Values in Italian Philosophy.**

38. W. H. Werkmeister, *Martin Heidegger on the Way*, edited by Richard T. Hull. A volume in **Werkmeister Studies.**

39. Phillip Stambovsky, *Myth and the Limits of Reason.*

40. Samantha Brennan, Tracy Isaacs, and Michael Milde, Editors, *A Question of Values: New Canadian Perspectives in Ethics and Political Philosophy.*

41. Peter A. Redpath, *Cartesian Nightmare: An Introduction to Transcendental Sophistry.* A volume in **Studies in the History of Western Philosophy.**

42. Clark Butler, *History as the Story of Freedom: Philosophy in Intercultural Context,* with Responses by sixteen scholars.

43. Dennis Rohatyn, *Philosophy History Sophistry.*

44. Leon Shaskolsky Sheleff, *Social Cohesion and Legal Coercion: A Critique of Weber, Durkheim, and Marx.* Afterword by Virginia Black.

45. Alan Soble, Editor, *Sex, Love, and Friendship: Studies of the Society for the Philosophy of Sex and Love, 1977-1992.* A volume in **Histories and Addresses of Philosophical Societies.**

46. Peter A. Redpath, *Wisdom's Odyssey: From Philosophy to Transcendental Sophistry.* A volume in **Studies in the History of Western Philosophy.**

47. Albert A. Anderson, *Universal Justice: A Dialectical Approach.* A volume in **Universal Justice.**

48. Pio Colonnello, *The Philosophy of Jose Gaos.* Translated from Italian by Peter Cocozzella. Edited by Myra Moss. Introduction by Giovanni Gullace. A volume in **Values in Italian Philosophy.**

65. Dane R. Gordon and Józef Niżnik, Editors, *Criticism and Defense of Rationality in Contemporary Philosophy*. A volume in **Post-Communist European Thought.**

66. John R. Shook, *Pragmatism: An Annotated Bibliography, 1898-1940.* With Contributions by E. Paul Colella, Lesley Friedman, Frank X. Ryan, and Ignas K. Skrupskelis.

67. Lansana Keita, *The Human Project and the Temptations of Science.*

68. Michael M. Kazanjian, *Phenomenology and Education: Cosmology, Co-Being, and Core Curriculum.* A volume in **Philosophy of Education.**

69. James W. Vice, *The Reopening of the American Mind: On Skepticism and Constitutionalism.*

70. Sarah Bishop Merrill, *Defining Personhood: Toward the Ethics of Quality in Clinical Care.*

71. Dane R. Gordon, *Philosophy and Vision.*

72. Alan Milchman and Alan Rosenberg, Editors, *Postmodernism and the Holocaust.* A volume in **Holocaust and Genocide Studies.**

73. Peter A. Redpath, *Masquerade of the Dream Walkers: Prophetic Theology from the Cartesians to Hegel.* A volume in **Studies in the History of Western Philosophy.**

74. Malcolm D. Evans, *Whitehead and Philosophy of Education: The Seamless Coat of Learning.* A volume in **Philosophy of Education.**

75. Warren E. Steinkraus, *Taking Religious Claims Seriously: A Philosophy of Religion*, edited by Michael H. Mitias. A volume in **Universal Justice.**

76. Thomas Magnell, Editor, *Values and Education.*

77. Kenneth A. Bryson, *Persons and Immortality.* A volume in **Natural Law Studies.**

78. Steven V. Hicks, *International Law and the Possibility of a Just World Order: An Essay on Hegel's Universalism.* A volume in **Universal Justice.**

79. E.F. Kaelin, *Texts on Texts and Textuality: A Phenomenology of Literary Art*, edited by Ellen J. Burns.

80. Amihud Gilead, *Saving Possibilities: A Study in Philosophical Psychology*, A volume in **Philosophy and Psychology**.

81. André Mineau, *The Making of the Holocaust: Ideology and Ethics in the Systems Perspective*. A volume in **Holocaust and Genocide Studies**.

82. Howard P. Kainz, *Politically Incorrect Dialogues: Topics Not Discussed in Polite Circles*.

83. Veikko Launis, Juhani Pietarinen, and Juha Räikkä, Editors, *Genes and Morality: New Essays*. A volume in **Nordic Value Studies**.

84. Steven Schroeder, *The Metaphysics of Cooperation: A Study of F. D. Maurice*.

85. Caroline Joan ("Kay") S. Picart, *Thomas Mann and Friedrich Nietzsche: Eroticism, Death, Music, and Laughter*. A volume in **Central-European Value Studies**.

86. G. John M. Abbarno, Editor, *The Ethics of Homelessness: Philosophical Perspectives*.

87. James Giles, Editor, *French Existentialism: Consciousness, Ethics, and Relations with Others*. A volume in **Nordic Value Studies**.

88. Deane Curtin and Robert Litke, Editors, *Institutional Violence*. A volume in **Philosophy of Peace**.

89. Yuval Lurie, *Cultural Beings: Reading the Philosophers of* Genesis.

90. Sandra A. Wawrytko, Editor, *The Problem of Evil: An Intercultural Exploration*. A volume in **Philosophy and Psychology**.

91. Gary J. Acquaviva, *Values, Violence, and Our Future*. A volume in **Hartman Institute Axiology Studies**.

92. Michael R. Rhodes, *Coercion: A Nonevaluative Approach*.

93. Jacques Kriel, *Matter, Mind, and Medicine: Transforming the Clinical Method*.

94. Haim Gordon, *Dwelling Poetically: Educational Challenges in Heidegger's Thinking on Poetry*. A volume in **Philosophy of Education**.

95. Ludwig Grünberg, *The Mystery of Values: Studies in Axiology*, edited by. Cornelia Grünberg, and Laura Grünberg.

Raising the Stakes

Raising the Stakes provides an understanding of the breadth of resources that are needed to provide a quality education to all students so that every individual, organisation and institution can become a stakeholder in the enterprise.

This comprehensive book draws on best practice in several countries to show how resources can be allocated to help achieve high expectations for all schools. The book demonstrates how schools can move from satisfaction with improvement to accepting the challenge to transform, identifying and exploring the need to align four kinds of resources:

- intellectual capital, that is, the knowledge and skill of talented professionals;
- social capital, being mutual support from networks of individuals, organisations, agencies and institutions in the broader community;
- financial capital, which must be carefully targeted to ensure that these resources are aligned and focused on priorities for learning;
- spiritual capital, which can be viewed in a religious sense or in terms of the culture and values that bring coherence and unity to these endeavours.

Practitioners and researchers reading this book will be inspired to work more closely in networking knowledge about how 'high quality' and 'high equity' can be achieved. *Raising the Stakes* is essential reading for those with the responsibility of ensuring that resources are acquired and allocated to achieve the best possible outcomes for students.

Brian J. Caldwell is managing director of Educational Transformations and a former Dean of Education at the University of Melbourne, Australia.

Jim M. Spinks is director of All Across the Line and a former School Principal who consults widely on student-focused planning and resource allocation. He is based in Australia.

This is the fourth book by Caldwell and Spinks following *The Self-Managing School* (1988), *Leading the Self-Managing School* (1992) and *Beyond the Self-Managing School* (1998).

Leading School Transformation series

Series Editors:

Alma Harris
University of Warwick, UK

Claire Mathews
Head of Leadership programmes, Specialist Schools and Academies Trust

Sue Williamson
Director of Leadership and Innovation, Specialist Schools and Academies Trust

The Leading School Transformation series brings together leading researchers and writers to identify the latest thinking about new and innovative leadership practices that transform schools and school systems. The books have been written with educational professionals in mind, and draw upon the latest international research and evidence to offer new ways of thinking about leadership; provide examples of leadership in practice and identify concrete ways of transforming leadership for schools and school systems in the future.

Forthcoming title:

Distributed Leadership in Schools
Developing tomorrow's leaders
Alma Harris